THE
GREAT BRITISH
PUB QUIZ
BOOK

This is a Carlton Book

This edition published in 2014 by
Carlton Books Limited
20 Mortimer Street
London W1T 3JW

ISBN 978-1-78097-579-5

1 3 5 7 9 10 8 6 4 2

Printed and bound by CPI Group (UK) Ltd, Croydon, CR0 4YY

Some of the material in this book was previously published in
The Biggest Pub Quiz Book Ever!

THE
GREAT BRITISH
PUB QUIZ
BOOK

**MORE THAN 1,000 QUESTIONS ABOUT
PEOPLE, PLACES, CUSTOMS AND CULTURE**

CARLTON
BOOKS

CONTENTS

INTRODUCTION

Welcome to this pub quiz book, based on all sorts of subjects that are popular in pub quizzes all over the British Isles.

This book is filled with questions (and their answers) about all sorts of subjects, from music and theatre to mountains and politics. There are questions for all sorts of abilities, so you should be able to enjoy yourself however old you are and wherever you come from. The people who will be able to answer most questions are those who have lived in the UK for the longest, or maybe those who have studied English for longest. But don't worry, all the questions are multiple choice so you will never be stuck for an answer!

Use this book as a quiz by yourself or with friends, as a source of information, or as a fun test of your general knowledge. Whatever you do, have fun.

Author's note: you may notice some questions in here that do not exclusively relate to the UK. If that's the case, they will relate to events or cultural references that are deeply ingrained in the UK and its population, so are very relevant in this book. So please, enjoy yourself, and look out for more books in the series!

QUIZ 1

1. Which type of calendar is used today in the western world?
- ☐ Berber
- ☐ Gregorian
- ☐ Islamic
- ☐ Jamesian

2. What instrument can be bass, electric or Spanish?
- ☐ Guitar
- ☐ Sitar
- ☐ Drums
- ☐ Violin

3. Which hurricane devastated New Orleans in September 2005?
- ☐ Katrina
- ☐ Erika
- ☐ Kate
- ☐ Katia

4. What do the numbers add up to on the opposite sides of a dice?
- ☐ 5
- ☐ 6
- ☐ 7
- ☐ 8

5. In the zodiac, which animal is linked with Capricorn?
- ☐ Ram
- ☐ Bull
- ☐ Goat
- ☐ Monkey

6. Which country originated the term "plonk" for wine?

- ☐ England
- ☐ France
- ☐ USA
- ☐ Australia

7. How many years are involved in a silver anniversary?

- ☐ 15
- ☐ 20
- ☐ 25
- ☐ 50

8. Which men used to perform with Ken Dodd?

- ☐ Button
- ☐ Diddy
- ☐ Oompa Loompas
- ☐ Northern

9. How many sides has a 20-pence piece?

- ☐ 5
- ☐ 7
- ☐ 9
- ☐ 1

10. What was Den's nickname in *EastEnders*?

- ☐ Big
- ☐ Dirty
- ☐ Hairy
- ☐ Honest

———————————————— ANSWERS

1 Gregorian. 2 Guitar. 3 Katrina 3. 4 7. 5 Goat. 6 Australia. 7 25. 8 Diddy. 9 7. 10 Dirty.

9

QUIZ 2: CELEBRITY

1. Which of these is the name of a TV show?
- ☐ Lion's Den
- ☐ Dragon's Den
- ☐ Denbigh Den
- ☐ Rat's Nest

2. Who beat Gareth Gates to win *Pop Idol*?
- ☐ Michelle McManus
- ☐ Darius Campbell
- ☐ Bill Young
- ☐ Will Young

3. Myleene Klass was part of which band?
- ☐ Girls Aloud
- ☐ Hear'Say
- ☐ Atomic Kitten
- ☐ All Saints

4. Which juror walked out of *The X Factor* in autumn 2005?
- ☐ Simon Cowell
- ☐ Sharon Osbourne
- ☐ Louis Walsh
- ☐ Kate Thornton

5. Rebekah Wade, then Mrs Ross Kemp, edited which paper when they made front-page news with assault allegations?
- ☐ The Sun
- ☐ The Times
- ☐ News of the World
- ☐ Private Eye

6. Which _X Factor_ celebrity is married to Ozzy Osbourne?

☐ Simon Cowell
☐ Sharon Osbourne
☐ Louis Walsh
☐ Kate Thornton

7. Which Ali was created by Sacha Baron Cohen?

☐ D
☐ E
☐ F
☐ G

8. Which Elizabeth did Gwyneth Paltrow replace as the face of Estee Lauder?

☐ Bates
☐ Hurley
☐ Taylor
☐ Windsor

9. Which Lawrence was a star of _Changing Rooms_?

☐ Bowen
☐ Gavin
☐ Llewelyn Bowen
☐ Ryder Richardson

10. Which antiques celebrity coined the phrase "cheap as chips"?

☐ David Dickinson
☐ Michael Hogben
☐ David Davies
☐ Tim Wonnacott

——————————— ANSWERS

1 Dragon's Den. 2 Will Young. 3 Hear'Say. 4 Louis Walsh. 5 The Sun. 6 Sharon Osbourne. 7 G. 8 Hurley. 9 Llewelyn Bowen. 10 David Dickinson.

11

QUIZ 3

1. What is the highest number used in a Sudoku puzzle?
- ☐ 6
- ☐ 7
- ☐ 8
- ☐ 9

2. What is the term for a positive electrode?
- ☐ Anode
- ☐ Diode
- ☐ Plectrode
- ☐ Plusser

3. Which swimming stroke is named after an insect?
- ☐ Breast
- ☐ Butterfly
- ☐ Dog paddle
- ☐ Trudgeon

4. Which English queen has the same name as a type of plum?
- ☐ Anne
- ☐ Elizabeth
- ☐ Jubilee
- ☐ Victoria

5. How many dots are used in each letter in the Braille system?
- ☐ Six
- ☐ Nine
- ☐ Twelve
- ☐ Fifteen

6. What is a female deer called?
- ☐ Buck
- ☐ Doe
- ☐ Fawn
- ☐ Rae

7. What does the letter B stand for in an ASBO?
- ☐ Badboy
- ☐ Barring
- ☐ Blame
- ☐ Behaviour

8. What can be an island, an article of clothing or a potato?
- ☐ Skye
- ☐ Jersey
- ☐ King Edward
- ☐ Maris Piper

9. What unit is used to measure horses?
- ☐ Feet
- ☐ Hands
- ☐ Metres
- ☐ Yards

10. Who is Reg Dwight better known as?
- ☐ Billy Joel
- ☐ Elton John
- ☐ Paul McCartney
- ☐ Bernie Taupin

ANSWERS

1 9. 2 Anode. 3 Butterfly. 4 Victoria. 5 Six. 6 Doe.
7 Behaviour. 8 Jersey. 9 Hands. 10 Elton John.

QUIZ 4

1. How many tenpin bowling skittles need knocking down for a strike?
☐ 9
☐ 10
☐ 11
☐ 12

2. How is 77 represented in Roman numerals?
☐ LIIIXXX
☐ LXVII
☐ MXXVII
☐ LXXVII

3. Who is the patron saint of music?
☐ Camilla
☐ Camille
☐ Cecilia
☐ Charles

4. What are birds of a feather said to do?
☐ Do time together
☐ Eat together
☐ Flock together
☐ Gather no moss

5. What is the only bird that can hover in the air and also fly backwards?
☐ Buzzard
☐ Hummingbird
☐ Kestrel
☐ Osprey

6. Who earned the nickname "Slow-hand"?
- [ ] Dan Brown
- [ ] Eric Clapton
- [ ] Chris de Burgh
- [ ] Chris Rea

7. How many sides has an octagon?
- [ ] 5
- [ ] 8
- [ ] 18
- [ ] 20

8. How many children were there in Enid Blyton's Famous Five?
- [ ] 3
- [ ] 4
- [ ] 5
- [ ] 6

9. What is the stage name of Harry Webb?
- [ ] Engelbert Humperdinck
- [ ] Tom Jones
- [ ] Cliff Richard
- [ ] Bruce Welch

10. Which season do Americans call the Fall?
- [ ] Spring
- [ ] Summer
- [ ] Autumn
- [ ] Winter

ANSWERS

1 10. 2 LXXVII. 3 Cecilia. 4 Flock together. 5 Hummingbird. 6 Eric Clapton.
7. 8. 8 4 – one was a dog. 9 Cliff Richard. 10 Autumn.

15

QUIZ 5

1. Who captained England to their Ashes win in 2005?
- ☐ Andrew Flintoff
- ☐ Kevin Pietersen
- ☐ Andrew Strauss
- ☐ Michael Vaughn

2. What colour is a sapphire?
- ☐ Blue
- ☐ Green
- ☐ Red
- ☐ Yellow

3. What did Bo and Luke Duke call their car?
- ☐ The Duke of Hazzard
- ☐ Daisy Duke
- ☐ The General Lee
- ☐ Uncle Jesse

4. In Shakespeare's *Othello*, who is the female lead?
- ☐ Desdemona
- ☐ Juliet
- ☐ Pandora
- ☐ Portia

5. In the pirate song, how many men were on the dead man's chest?
- ☐ 5
- ☐ 10
- ☐ 15
- ☐ 20

6. A poult is the young of which creature?

☐ Chicken
☐ Deer
☐ Duck
☐ Turkey

7. In an English trial, how many people sit on the jury?

☐ 9
☐ 10
☐ 11
☐ 12

8. In which game do you draw part of a gallows for every wrong answer?

☐ Cluedo
☐ Hangman
☐ Noughts and crosses
☐ Scrabble

9. Bright's disease affects which part of the body?

☐ Heart
☐ Kidneys
☐ Liver
☐ Stomach

10. Which actress said, "I want to be alone"?

☐ Joan Crawford
☐ Bette Davis
☐ Marlene Dietrich
☐ Greta Garbo

ANSWERS

1 Michael Vaughn. 2 Blue. 3 General Lee. 4 Desdemona. 5 15. 6 Turkey. 7 12. 8 Hangman. 9 Kidneys. 10 Greta Garbo.

17

QUIZ 6: 1950S MUSIC

1. What was the name of Bill Haley's backing group?
- [ ] The Comets
- [ ] The Crickets
- [ ] The Shadows
- [ ] The Young Ones

2. What kind of doll was Cliff Richard's first No 1?
- [ ] Baby
- [ ] Living
- [ ] Loving
- [ ] Plastic

3. Where was the Doggie when Lita Roza asked how much it was?
- [ ] In the pet shop
- [ ] In the window
- [ ] In the park
- [ ] In the pet cemetery

4. What relation to each other were Don and Phil Everly?
- [ ] Brothers
- [ ] Father and son
- [ ] None
- [ ] Uncle and nephew

5. Where were the tulips from, which Max Bygraves sang about?
- [ ] Aberdeen
- [ ] Amstelveen
- [ ] Amsterdam
- [ ] Arnhem

6. Which line follows "Be Bop A Lula" at the start of the Gene Vincent hit?

☐ She's a baby

☐ She's my baby

☐ She'd be a baby

☐ I don't mean maybe

7. How many steps are there to heaven?

☐ 1

☐ 3

☐ 5

☐ 7

8. According to Lonnie Donegan what might lose its flavour on the bedpost overnight?

☐ Cheese

☐ Chewing gum

☐ Denture cream

☐ Wax

9. How many tons did Tennessee Ernie Ford sing about?

☐ 10

☐ 12

☐ 14

☐ 16

10. According to the Platters what gets in your eyes?

☐ Blood

☐ Paint

☐ Smoke

☐ Tears

ANSWERS

1 Comets. 2 Living Charles. 3 In the window. 4 Brothers. 5 Amsterdam. 6 She's my baby. 7 3. 8 Chewing gum. 9 16. 10 Smoke.

19

QUIZ 7

1. How many stomachs has a cow?
- [ ] 1
- [ ] 2
- [ ] 3
- [ ] 4

2. What have you been doing if you finish by casting off?
- [ ] Fishing
- [ ] Knitting
- [ ] Ice Fishing
- [ ] Macramé

3. How is the Roman city of Verulamium known today?
- [ ] Bath
- [ ] Colchester
- [ ] London
- [ ] St Albans

4. Which city in the world has the largest population?
- [ ] Jakarta
- [ ] Mexico City
- [ ] Seoul
- [ ] Tokyo

5. Whose ship was the first to sail round the world?
- [ ] Christopher Columbus
- [ ] Vasco da Gama
- [ ] Ferdinand Magellan
- [ ] Marco Polo

6. Who composed "The Flight of the Bumble Bee"?

- [ ] Mussorgsky
- [ ] Rimsky-Korsakov
- [ ] Rachmaninov
- [ ] Tchaikovsky

7. What was invented by Lewis Waterman in the 1880s?

- [ ] Computer
- [ ] Fountain pen
- [ ] Flushing toilet
- [ ] Windmill

8. Which instrument usually has 47 strings?

- [ ] Guitar
- [ ] Harp
- [ ] Harpsichord
- [ ] Piano

9.What is the name of Dennis the Menace's dog?

- [ ] Buster
- [ ] Chomper
- [ ] Gnasher
- [ ] Snoopy

10. Moving anti-clockwise on a dartboard what is the number next to 4?

- [ ] 16
- [ ] 17
- [ ] 18
- [ ] 19

ANSWERS

1 4. 2 Knitting. 3 St Albans. 4 Tokyo. 5 Magellan. 6 Rimsky-Korsakov. 7 Fountain pen. 8 Harp. 9 Gnasher. 10 18.

QUIZ 8

1. How many more letters are there in the English than the Greek alphabet?

☐ 1
☐ 2
☐ 3
☐ 4

2. Which food item is used in an annual race at Olney?

☐ Banana
☐ Cheese
☐ Oranges
☐ Pancakes

3. In legend, who slew the gorgon Medusa?

☐ Argos
☐ Jason
☐ Perses
☐ Perseus

4. How many legs has a lobster?

☐ 4
☐ 6
☐ 8
☐ 10

5. Louise Brown will always hold which famous first?

☐ Cloned human
☐ First female politician in England
☐ Last woman to be executed in England
☐ Test tube baby

6. On the radio where are you sent with eight records of your choice?

☐ Desert island
☐ Hell
☐ Outer space
☐ Room 101

7. Which part of its body does a snake use to smell?

☐ Ears
☐ Eyelashes
☐ Tip of tail
☐ Tongue

8. Which magazine has been edited by Richard Ingrams and Ian Hislop?

☐ Private Eye
☐ Punch
☐ Radio Times
☐ The Week

9. In which country was Checkpoint Charlie located?

☐ England
☐ France
☐ (West) Germany
☐ Vietnam

10. What number in bingo is two fat ladies?

☐ 11
☐ 22
☐ 66
☐ 88

— ANSWERS

1 2. 2 Pancakes. 3 Perseus. 4 10. 5 First test tube baby. 6 Desert Island. 7 Tongue. 8 Private Eye. 9 West Germany. 10 88.

QUIZ 9

1. How many notes are there in an octave?

☐ 7
☐ 8
☐ 9
☐ 10

2. What does an arctophile collect?

☐ Art
☐ Spiders
☐ Stamps
☐ Teddy bears

3. Which of Verdi's operas is set in Ancient Egypt?

☐ Aida
☐ La Traviata
☐ Macbeth
☐ Rigoletto

4. What gives red blood cells their colour?

☐ Erythrocytes
☐ Father Christmas
☐ Haemoglobin
☐ Platelets

5. On TV, what kind of creature was Flipper?

☐ Cat
☐ Dog
☐ Dolphin
☐ Seal

6. What is the main ingredient in a brick?

☐ Clay
☐ Concrete
☐ Dust
☐ Mud

7. What is the body of a penguin covered with?

☐ Feathers
☐ Fur
☐ Hair
☐ Scales

8. How is the auracaria tree more commonly known?

☐ Acacia
☐ Birch
☐ Monkey puzzle
☐ Strawberry tree

9. How does Saturday's child work for a living?

☐ Hard
☐ Long
☐ Slowly
☐ With joy

10. Which bell said, "You owe me five farthings"?

☐ Bow
☐ Old Bailey
☐ St Martins
☐ St Stephen

ANSWERS

1 8. 2 Teddy bears. 3 Aida. 4 Haemoglobin. 5 Dolphin. 6 Clay. 7 Feathers. 8 Monkey puzzle. 9 Hard. 10 St Martins.

25

QUIZ 10: 60S SOUNDS

1. What was the occupation of Lonnie Donegan's old man?
- ☐ Chewing gum cleaner
- ☐ Dustman
- ☐ Footballer
- ☐ Postman

2. In which part of town was Petula Clark in the 1960s?
- ☐ Down
- ☐ Bad
- ☐ Mid-
- ☐ Up

3. What shade of Pale did Procol Harum sing about?
- ☐ Brighter
- ☐ Cleaner
- ☐ Darker
- ☐ Whiter

4. Who was Gerry's backing group?
- ☐ Gerrymanders
- ☐ Heartstoppers
- ☐ Pacemakers
- ☐ Walkers

5. What followed Ready, Steady in the title of the pop show?
- ☐ Go
- ☐ Pop
- ☐ Stop
- ☐ Weekend

6. Which group wrote the rock opera *Tommy*?

☐ Beatles
☐ Led Zeppelin
☐ The Troggs
☐ The Who

7. What colour was the Beatles' Submarine?

☐ Blue
☐ Green
☐ Orange
☐ Yellow

8. Who was heard to "Shout" in 1964?

☐ Cilla Black
☐ Petula Clark
☐ Lulu
☐ Sandie Shaw

9. Which famous team wrote "I Wanna Be Your Man" for the Rolling Stones?

☐ Lennon/McCartney
☐ Jagger/Richards
☐ Chuck Berry
☐ Holland/Dozier/Holland

10. How many were there in the Tops, Pennies and Seasons?

☐ Two
☐ Three
☐ Four
☐ Five

ANSWERS

1 Dustman. 2 Down. 3 Whiter. 4 Pacemakers. 5 Go. 6 The Who.
7 Yellow. 8 Lulu. 9 Lennon/McCartney. 10 Four.

27

QUIZ 11

1. Who had a No 1 hit with the song "Wuthering Heights"?
- ☐ Tori Amos
- ☐ Jane Austen
- ☐ Bjork
- ☐ Kate Bush

2. With which branch of medicine is Mesmer associated?
- ☐ Fertility
- ☐ Hypnotism
- ☐ Psychology
- ☐ Surgery

3. In the nursery rhyme, what did Tom, Tom the piper's son steal?
- ☐ A cake
- ☐ A march
- ☐ A pig
- ☐ Three blind mice

4. According to the proverb, what begins at home?
- ☐ Charity
- ☐ Faith
- ☐ Hope
- ☐ Patience

5. Who played TV's Inspector Morse?
- ☐ Colin Dexter
- ☐ John Thaw
- ☐ Dennis Waterman
- ☐ Kevin Whately

6. Which day of the week is named after the god Thor?

☐ Tuesday
☐ Wednesday
☐ Thursday
☐ Sunday

7. In the song, what did my true love send to me on the seventh day of Christmas?

☐ Five gold ring
☐ Six geese a-laying
☐ Seven swans a-swimming
☐ Seven pipers piping

8. Who was the famous son of Uther Pendragon?

☐ Arthur
☐ Gawain
☐ Lancelot
☐ Merlin

9. What was the most famous group managed by Andrew Loog Oldham?

☐ Beatles
☐ Rolling Stones
☐ Roxy Music
☐ Small Faces

10. Which English king was said to be Unready?

☐ Cnut the Great
☐ Edward
☐ Ethelred
☐ Uther

ANSWERS

1 Kate Bush. 2 Hypnotism. 3 A pig. 4 Charity. 5 John Thaw. 6 Thursday. 7 Seven swans a-swimming. 8 Arthur. 9 Rolling Stones. 10 Ethelred.

29

QUIZ 12

1. David Lean's film was about a passage to which country?
- ☐ Africa
- ☐ France
- ☐ India
- ☐ Narnia

2. According to a Nick Berry song title every loser does what?
- ☐ Dies poor
- ☐ Dies happy
- ☐ Loses
- ☐ Wins

3. How many sides has a parallelogram?
- ☐ 4
- ☐ 5
- ☐ 6
- ☐ 7

4. What nationality was the notorious murderer Dr Crippen?
- ☐ American
- ☐ Canadian
- ☐ English
- ☐ Welsh

5. In which TV programme do Patsy and Edina appear?
- ☐ Absolutely Fabulous
- ☐ French & Saunders
- ☐ Not the 9 o'clock News
- ☐ The Vicar of Dibley

6. In which month does the grouse shooting season start in Britain?

☐ June
☐ July
☐ August
☐ September

7. How many years are celebrated by a platinum anniversary?

☐ 25
☐ 50
☐ 70
☐ 75

8. In which month is Twelfth Night?

☐ January
☐ February
☐ August
☐ December

9. In the book title, whom did writer Laurie Lee have cider with?

☐ Rose
☐ Rosa
☐ Rosie
☐ Roz

10. Which musical does "I Know Him So Well" come from?

☐ Chess
☐ Mama Mia
☐ Once
☐ Phantom of the Opera

ANSWERS

1 India. 2 Wins. 3 4. 4 American. 5 Absolutely Fabulous. 6 August. 7 70. 8 January. 9 Rosie. 10 Chess.

31

QUIZ 13

1. In which country is Hampden Park Stadium?
☐ England
☐ Ireland
☐ Scotland
☐ Wales

2. Who made up Abba with Benny, Bjorn and Annifrid?
☐ Agnetha
☐ Anita
☐ Andy
☐ Anja

3. Which traveller had the unusual first name of Lemuel?
☐ Fogg
☐ Gulliver
☐ Polo
☐ Swift

4. Which Pharrell was 'Happy'?
☐ Gru
☐ Rodgers
☐ Thicke
☐ Williams

5. What do the French words au revoir mean?
☐ Goodbye
☐ Hello
☐ Please
☐ Thank you

6. Who said, "Am I dying beyond my means?"?

☐ Winston Churchill
☐ Charles Dickens
☐ Edgar Allen Poe
☐ Oscar Wilde

7. A car with the international registration letter E comes from where?

☐ Estonia
☐ Europe
☐ Spain
☐ Switzerland

8. Which army commander was known as "The Desert Fox"?

☐ Himler
☐ Montgomery
☐ Patton
☐ Rommel

9. In which city in 1916 was the Easter Rising?

☐ Belfast
☐ Dublin
☐ Galway
☐ Limerick

10. "Walk upon England's mountains green" is the second line of which rousing song?

☐ God Save the Queen
☐ Jerusalem
☐ The Stately Homes of England
☐ Vindaloo

ANSWERS

1 Scotland. 2 Agnetha. 3 Gulliver. 4 Williams. 5 Goodbye. 6 Oscar Wilde. 7 Spain. 8 Rommel. 9 Dublin. 10 Jerusalem.

33

QUIZ 14: THE NATURAL

1. What type of creature is a black widow?
- ☐ Cat
- ☐ Dog
- ☐ Snake
- ☐ Spider

2. Which animal's nickname is "ship of the desert"?
- ☐ Camel
- ☐ Desert Fox
- ☐ Scorpion
- ☐ Whale

3. Which breed of spaniel shares its name with a king?
- ☐ Cocker
- ☐ Henry VIII
- ☐ Kinger
- ☐ King Charles

4. What is a female sheep called?
- ☐ Doe
- ☐ Ewe
- ☐ Hen
- ☐ Sow

5. What do carnivorous animals live on?
- ☐ Fish
- ☐ Meat
- ☐ Trees
- ☐ Vegetables

6. What is a fox's tail called?

☐ Basil
☐ Brush
☐ Puffer
☐ Swisher

7. What would a billy and a nanny produce?

☐ Calf
☐ Child
☐ Kid
☐ Lamb

8. What does an Isle of Man Manx cat NOT have?

☐ Ears
☐ Fur
☐ Tail
☐ Two cars

9. What kind of animal is a Suffolk Punch?

☐ Cat
☐ Dog
☐ Horse
☐ Pony

10. A coalition is a group of which animals?

☐ Cheetah
☐ Chinchilla
☐ Coyote
☐ Echidna

ANSWERS

1 Spider. 2 Camel. 3 King Charles. 4 Ewe. 5 Meat. 6 Brush.
7 Kid (baby goat). 8 Tail. 9 Horse. 10 Cheetah.

35

QUIZ 15

1. Who wrote "The Owl and the Pussycat"?
- [ ] Lewis Carroll
- [ ] Edward Lear
- [ ] JK Rowling
- [ ] Alfred Tennyson

2. What are beds of snooker tables traditionally made of?
- [ ] Baize
- [ ] Chipboard
- [ ] Fuzzy felt
- [ ] Slate

3. What was the name of the *Neighbours* character played by Kylie Minogue?
- [ ] Charlene
- [ ] Chloe
- [ ] Coco
- [ ] Kylie

4.The Star of Africa is what type of gem?
- [ ] Diamond
- [ ] Emerald
- [ ] Ruby
- [ ] Sapphire

5. In education, what does BA stand for?
- [ ] Batchelor of Arts
- [ ] Best Artist
- [ ] Bright Academic
- [ ] Brighton Art College

6. What is arachnophobia the fear of?

☐ Flowers
☐ People
☐ Spiders
☐ Wolves

7. Which two writers created *Auf Wiedersehen, Pet*?

☐ Clement & La Frenais
☐ Croft & Lloyd
☐ Nail & Pace
☐ Perry & Croft

8. Under what name did Samuel Clemens write?

☐ Lewis Carroll
☐ Charles Dickens
☐ Ernest Hemingway
☐ Mark Twain

9. Who recorded the album *Tubular Bells*?

☐ Jean-Michelle Jarre
☐ Mike Oldfield
☐ Rush
☐ Rick Wakeman

10. Which day of the week is named after the moon?

☐ Friday
☐ Saturday
☐ Sunday
☐ Monday

ANSWERS

1 Edward Lear. 2 Slate. 3 Charlene. 4 Diamond. 5 Batchelor of Arts.
6 Spiders. 7 Clement & La Frenais. 8 Mark Twain. 9 Mike Oldfield. 10 Monday.

37

QUIZ 16

1. Jennyanydots was what kind of cat?
- [ ] Gumbie
- [ ] Jellicle
- [ ] Peke
- [ ] Pollicle

2. Who wrote *Rebecca*?
- [ ] Jane Austen
- [ ] Daphne du Maurier
- [ ] Joan Fontaine
- [ ] Lucy Maud

3. Who recorded the album *Definitely, Maybe*?
- [ ] Blur
- [ ] Oasis
- [ ] Stone Roses
- [ ] The Verve

4. In rhyming slang what is meant by dickory dock?
- [ ] Clock
- [ ] Frock
- [ ] Rock
- [ ] Sock

5. Which comedy series featured the Boswell family?
- [ ] Bread
- [ ] Butterflies
- [ ] The Royle Family
- [ ] The Thorn Birds

6. Whose catchphrase was, "Shut that door!"?
- ☐ Jim Bowen
- ☐ Ronnie Corbett
- ☐ Bruce Forsyth
- ☐ Larry Grayson

7. Which major river flows through Newcastle?
- ☐ Tees
- ☐ Tyne
- ☐ Tipple
- ☐ Trent

8. Who created Biggles?
- ☐ Richmal Crompton
- ☐ Enid Blyton
- ☐ Captain W E Johns
- ☐ James Bigglesworth

9. Which soccer side has Alexandra in its name?
- ☐ Crewe Alexandra
- ☐ Aston Alexandra
- ☐ Alexandra Palace
- ☐ Alexandra Hotspur

10. Name the missing member of One Direction: Harry, Zayn, Niall, Liam
- ☐ James
- ☐ Leon
- ☐ Louis
- ☐ Tom

ANSWERS

1 Gumbie. 2 Daphne du Maurier. 3 Oasis. 4 Clock. 5 Bread. 6 Larry Grayson. 7 Tyne. 8 Capt W E Johns. 9 Crewe Alexandra. 10 Lewis.

39

QUIZ 17

1. Which of the following colours is NOT in the flag of Belgium?
- ☐ Black
- ☐ Red
- ☐ White
- ☐ Yellow

2. What was the name of Miss Rigby in the song by the Beatles?
- ☐ Anna
- ☐ Eleanor
- ☐ Ellie
- ☐ Rita

3. In which city is the Oval cricket ground?
- ☐ London
- ☐ Manchester
- ☐ Nottingham
- ☐ Oval

4. Which Frederick wrote *The Day of the Jackal*?
- ☐ Forsyth
- ☐ LeCarré
- ☐ Ludlum
- ☐ Valentich

5. Which term means related to the moon?
- ☐ Linux
- ☐ Lunar
- ☐ Moonish
- ☐ Solar

6. Which Florence was known as the lady with the lamp?
- ☐ Benjamin
- ☐ Nightingale
- ☐ Nighy
- ☐ Seacole

7. What name refers to a young fox?
- ☐ Cub
- ☐ Pup
- ☐ Reynard
- ☐ Vixen

8. Which special name is given to a group of ravens?
- ☐ Bunch
- ☐ Crash
- ☐ Gaze
- ☐ Unkindness

9. C is the symbol of which chemical element?
- ☐ Carbon
- ☐ Calcium
- ☐ Copper
- ☐ Cobalt

10. Euclid is associated with which branch of mathematics?
- ☐ Algebra
- ☐ Calculus
- ☐ Geometry
- ☐ Number theory

—————— ANSWERS

1 White. 2 Eleanor. 3 London. 4 Forsyth. 5 Lunar. 6 Nightingale. 7 Pup. 8 Unkindness. 9 Carbon. 10 Geometry.

41

QUIZ 18: GEOGRAPHY

1. In which Swiss mountain range is the Jungfrau?
- ☐ Alps
- ☐ Andes
- ☐ Dolomites
- ☐ Jura

2. Which is the next largest island in the world after Australia?
- ☐ Borneo
- ☐ Greenland
- ☐ Madagascar
- ☐ New Guinea

3. Which of these is the odd one out?
- ☐ Chicago
- ☐ Erie
- ☐ Huron
- ☐ Ontario

4. If you were in Benidorm in which country would you be?
- ☐ Gibraltar
- ☐ Morocco
- ☐ Portugal
- ☐ Spain

5. Which Queen gave her name to the capital of Hong Kong?
- ☐ Anne
- ☐ Elizabeth
- ☐ Margaret
- ☐ Victoria

6. In which county is Penzance?

☐ Avon
☐ Cornwall
☐ Devon
☐ Dorset

7. What are the counties of Essex, Suffolk, Norfolk and Cambridgeshire collectively known as?

☐ East Anglia
☐ Home Counties
☐ The North
☐ Wales

8. f you were looking at the Ganges which country would you be in?

☐ Afghanistan
☐ India
☐ Pakistan
☐ Sri Lanka

9. Which country originally produced Fiat cars?

☐ France
☐ Germany
☐ Italy
☐ Spain

10. What is the most westerly point of England?

☐ Land's End
☐ The Lizard
☐ St David's Point
☐ Tralee

——————————— ANSWERS

1 Alps. 2 Greenland 3 Chicago (the others are 'great lakes'). 4 Spain. 5 Victoria. 6 Cornwall. 7 East Anglia. 8 India. 9 Italy. 10 Land's End.

43

QUIZ 19

1. How many players are there in a volleyball team?
- [ ] 6
- [ ] 7
- [ ] 8
- [ ] 9

2. In rhyming slang what is meant by rabbit and pork?
- [ ] Chalk
- [ ] Fork
- [ ] Meat
- [ ] Talk

3. What is the common name for the complaint bursitis?
- [ ] Housemaid's knee
- [ ] Tennis elbow
- [ ] Golfer's elbow
- [ ] Headache

4. In which city is La Scala opera house?
- [ ] Milan
- [ ] Naples
- [ ] Rome
- [ ] Venice

5. In the British army which rank comes between Lieutenant and Major?
- [ ] Captain
- [ ] Colonel
- [ ] Corporal
- [ ] First Lieutenant

6. What colour is the gem jet?
- [ ] Black
- [ ] Light blue
- [ ] Dark blue
- [ ] White

7. How many sides has a heptagon?
- [ ] 5
- [ ] 7
- [ ] 9
- [ ] 11

8. What type of creature is used for the dish Bombay duck?
- [ ] Chicken
- [ ] Duck
- [ ] Fish
- [ ] Lamb

9. What is the capital of Egypt?
- [ ] Alexandria
- [ ] Cairo
- [ ] Giza
- [ ] Suez

10. Which vegetable is also known as the egg plant?
- [ ] Aubergine
- [ ] Cabbage
- [ ] Swede
- [ ] Turnip

ANSWERS

1 6. 2 Talk. 3 Housemaid's knee. 4 Milan. 5 Captain. 6. Black. 7 7. 8 Fish. 9 Cairo. 10 Aubergine.

QUIZ 20

1. Dr John Pemberton invented which drink in 1886?
- ☐ Coca-Cola
- ☐ Champagne
- ☐ Tab
- ☐ Irn-Bru

2. What is the Welsh name for Wales?
- ☐ Croeso
- ☐ Cymru
- ☐ Gwael
- ☐ Nag oes

3. Who directed the film *Tommy*?
- ☐ Ken Loach
- ☐ Oliver Reed
- ☐ Ken Russell
- ☐ Pete Townshend

4. The Haka is a dance performed by which rugby union team?
- ☐ Australia (Wallabies)
- ☐ Argentina (Pumas)
- ☐ New Zealand (All-blacks)
- ☐ South Africa (Springboks)

5. On what part of your body would you wear espadrilles?
- ☐ Feet
- ☐ Hands
- ☐ Head
- ☐ Neck

6. What does the French word "pomme" mean?

☐ Apple
☐ Cheese
☐ Roast beef
☐ Wine

7. Who wrote the poem "Anthem for Doomed Youth"?

☐ Rupert Brooke
☐ Wilfred Owen
☐ Isaac Rosenberg
☐ Siegfried Sassoon

8. Which writer featured Jonathan Harker in his most famous novel?

☐ Charles Dickens
☐ Mary Shelley
☐ Robert Louis Stevenson
☐ Bram Stoker

9. How many legs has a spider?

☐ 6
☐ 8
☐ 9
☐ 10

10. In music, name the horizontal lines around which notes are written.

☐ Bar
☐ Clef
☐ Stave
☐ Stove

ANSWERS

6 Apple. 7 Wilfred Owen. 8 Bram Stoker. 9 8. 10 Stave.
1 Coca Cola. 2 Cymru. 3 Ken Russell. 4 New Zealand. 5 Feet.

47

QUIZ 21

1. In the story, how many men were in Jerome K. Jerome's boat?
- ☐ 1
- ☐ 2
- ☐ 3
- ☐ 4

2. In 1930, which country did Amy Johnson fly to from England?
- ☐ Australia
- ☐ France
- ☐ South Africa
- ☐ USA

3. What meat appears in a Punch and Judy show?
- ☐ Bacon
- ☐ Roast beef
- ☐ Sausages
- ☐ Steak

4. Who was the tallest of Robin Hood's Men?
- ☐ Big John
- ☐ Friar Tuck
- ☐ Little John
- ☐ Will Scarlet

5. Sol Campbell joined Arsenal from which club?
- ☐ Chelsea
- ☐ Manchester United
- ☐ Rotherham
- ☐ Tottenham Hotspur

6. Who wrote the song "White Christmas"?

- [ ] Irving Berlin
- [ ] Bing Crosby
- [ ] George Gershwin
- [ ] Cole Porter

7. In which English town did Charles and Camilla marry?

- [ ] London
- [ ] Slough
- [ ] Truro
- [ ] Windsor

8. Who composed "Peter Grimes"?

- [ ] Benjamin Britten
- [ ] Peter Grimes
- [ ] Peter Pears
- [ ] John Shirley-Quirk

9. What does PAYE stand for?

- [ ] Pay and you eat
- [ ] Pay as you earn
- [ ] Plan and you execute
- [ ] Pull and you enter

10. What is the name of the pub in Albert Square?

- [ ] Queen of Hearts
- [ ] Queen's Head
- [ ] Queen Victoria
- [ ] Red Lion

ANSWERS
1 3. 2 Australia. 3 Sausages. 4 Little John. 5 Tottenham Hotspur.
6 Irving Berlin. 7 Windsor. 8 Benjamin Britten. 9 Pay as you earn. 10 Queen Victoria.

49

QUIZ 22: SPORT

1. In tennis, what is a score of 40 all called?

☐ 40-love

☐ 40-something

☐ Deuce

☐ Tiebreak

2. Which Gary was England's top soccer marksman of the 1980s?

☐ Gascoigne

☐ Hansen

☐ Lineker

☐ Owen

3. Which club were English soccer champions six times in the 80s?

☐ Arsenal

☐ Liverpool

☐ Manchester City

☐ Manchester United

4. Which motor-cycle legend Mike was killed in a motor accident in 1981?

☐ Essex

☐ Hailwood

☐ Sheene

☐ Surtees

5. Which team won the FA Cup in 2013?

☐ Chelsea

☐ Manchester United

☐ Manchester City

☐ Wigan Athletic

6. Which country beat West Germany to win the 1982 soccer World Cup?

☐ East Germany
☐ Italy
☐ Mexico
☐ Spain

7. Who won Wimbledon men's singles in 2013?

☐ Roger Federer
☐ Andy Murray
☐ Rafael Nadal
☐ Novak Djokovic

8. Which country is Formula One's Fernando Alonso from?

☐ Argentina
☐ Italy
☐ Spain
☐ UK

9. What was Barry McGuigan's sport?

☐ Boxing
☐ Football
☐ Horse riding
☐ Wrestling

10. Which football team had UNICEF on their shirts for six years?

☐ Atletico Madrid
☐ Brugge FC
☐ FC Barcelona
☐ Chelsea

ANSWERS

1 Deuce. 2 Lineker. 3 Liverpool. 4 Hailwood. 5 Wigan. 6 Italy. 7 Murray. 8 Spain. 9 Boxing. 10 Barcelona.

51

QUIZ 23

1. Which rock superstar is a former chairman of Watford football club?
- [ ] Noel Gallagher
- [ ] Elton John
- [ ] Cliff Richard
- [ ] Robbie Williams

2. In which month is Royal Ascot horse-racing season?
- [ ] April
- [ ] May
- [ ] June
- [ ] July

3. What type of food is dill?
- [ ] Herb
- [ ] Mineral
- [ ] Spice
- [ ] Seed

4. On what date is American Independence Day?
- [ ] June 4
- [ ] July 4
- [ ] September 1
- [ ] December 25

5. What kind of animal is a seahorse?
- [ ] Arachnid
- [ ] Fish
- [ ] Invertebrate
- [ ] Mammal

6. Which insect transmits malaria?

- ☐ Ant
- ☐ Mealybug
- ☐ Mosquito
- ☐ Tsetse fly

7. In the fable, what did the boy cry to trick the villagers?

- ☐ Help!
- ☐ Murder!
- ☐ Thief!
- ☐ Wolf?

8. During which war was *Dad's Army* set?

- ☐ Boer War
- ☐ Korean War
- ☐ World War I
- ☐ World War II

9. Which country is Lufthansa from?

- ☐ Belgium
- ☐ France
- ☐ Germany
- ☐ Switzerland

10. In 2005 Tim Burton's directed a movie based on a folk tale about what type of "Bride"?

- ☐ Blushing
- ☐ Corpse
- ☐ Old
- ☐ Virgin

ANSWERS

1 Elton John. 2 June. 3 Herb. 4 July 4. 5 Fish. 6 Mosquito. 7 Wolf. 8 World War II. 9 Germany. 10. Corpse.

53

QUIZ 24

1. In Morse Code what letter is represented by three dashes?
- ☐ A
- ☐ E
- ☐ O
- ☐ S

2. In rhyming slang what are mince pies?
- ☐ Cakes
- ☐ Ears
- ☐ Eyes
- ☐ Pasties

3. How is Frances Gumm better known?
- ☐ Judy Garland
- ☐ Vicki Lester
- ☐ Liza Minnelli
- ☐ Shirley Temple

4. In which branch of the arts is the metronome used?
- ☐ Dance
- ☐ Music
- ☐ Painting
- ☐ Theatre

5. Which musical instrument featured in the theme of *The Third Man*?
- ☐ Balalaika
- ☐ Guitar
- ☐ Lute
- ☐ Zither

6. What colour is vermilion?

- [ ] Blue
- [ ] Green
- [ ] Red
- [ ] Yellow

7. Which member of the Rolling Stones is the movie _Stoned_ about?

- [ ] Mick Jagger
- [ ] Brian Jones
- [ ] Keith Richards
- [ ] Charlie Watts

8. How many sides has a decagon?

- [ ] 8
- [ ] 10
- [ ] 12
- [ ] 13

9. A cob is a male of which creature?

- [ ] Cow
- [ ] Donkey
- [ ] Elephant
- [ ] Horse

10. From which fish is caviar obtained?

- [ ] Cod
- [ ] Salmon
- [ ] Sturgeon
- [ ] Whitefish

ANSWERS

1 O. 2 Eyes. 3 Judy Garland 5. 4 Music. 5 Zither. 6 Red 4. 7 Brian Jones. 8 10. 9 Horse. 10 Sturgeon.

55

QUIZ 25

1. What is the capital of Belgium?
- ☐ Antwerp
- ☐ Bruges
- ☐ Brussels
- ☐ Ghent

2. Which mountain was said to be home of the Greek gods?
- ☐ Hades
- ☐ Mountains of the Moon
- ☐ Olympus
- ☐ Sparta

3. If it rains on St Swithin's Day, how many more days is it supposed to rain?
- ☐ 10
- ☐ 20
- ☐ 30
- ☐ 40

4. Which composer wrote *The Marriage of Figaro*?
- ☐ Beethoven
- ☐ Don Giovanni
- ☐ Mozart
- ☐ Verdo

5. In which month is Remembrance Day?
- ☐ September
- ☐ October
- ☐ November
- ☐ December

6. What are the initials of "Lady Chatterley" author Lawrence?

- [ ] DH
- [ ] HD
- [ ] JRR
- [ ] RR

7. What name is given to a litter of piglets?

- [ ] Brood
- [ ] Clutch
- [ ] Farrow
- [ ] Snort

8. Who recorded the album *Both Sides*?

- [ ] Phil Collins
- [ ] Peter Gabriel
- [ ] Steve Hackett
- [ ] Mike Rutherford

9. How many children did Queen Victoria have?

- [ ] 1
- [ ] 2
- [ ] 3
- [ ] 9

10. Who is the resident Lord in *Private Eye*?

- [ ] Cook
- [ ] Fraud
- [ ] Gnome
- [ ] Hislop

ANSWERS

10 Gnome.

1 Brussels. 2 Olympus. 3 40. 4 Mozart. 5 November. 6 DH. 7 Farrow. 8 Phil Collins. 9 9.

57

QUIZ 26: LITERATURE

1. Who created the character of Miss Marple?
☐ Agatha Christie
☐ Arthur Conan Doyle
☐ Page and Plant
☐ Dorothy L. Sayers

2. Whose first Secret Diary was written when he was 13 ¾?
☐ Adrian Cole
☐ Aidan Mole
☐ Adrian Mole
☐ Adrian Townshend

3. What was the profession of James Herriot?
☐ Author
☐ Doctor
☐ Dustman
☐ Vet

4. Which London barrister was created by John Mortimer?
☐ Kavanagh
☐ Lovejoy
☐ Morse
☐ Rumpole

5. Which Ruth created Inspector Wexford?
☐ Highsmith
☐ James
☐ Rendell
☐ Reynolds

6. What did Tolstoy write about together with War?

☐ Cakes
☐ Love
☐ Peace
☐ Politics

7. Which bird of prey Has Landed, in the book by Jack Higgins?

☐ Buzzard
☐ Eagle
☐ Kite
☐ Vulture

8. How many Musketeers were there in the title of the book by Dumas?

☐ 2
☐ 3
☐ 4
☐ 5

9. Which popular yellow spring flower did Wordsworth write about?

☐ Anemone
☐ Crocus
☐ Daffodil
☐ Iris

10. What is the nationality of Agatha Christie's detective Poirot?

☐ Belgian
☐ French
☐ German
☐ Irish

ANSWERS

1 Agatha Christie. 2 Adrian Mole. 3 Vet. 4 Rumpole. 5 Rendell. 6 Peace. 7 Eagle. 8 3. 9 Daffodil. 10 Belgian.

QUIZ 27

1. How many seconds in five minutes?
- ☐ 240
- ☐ 250
- ☐ 280
- ☐ 300

2. Which country hosted the last World Cup of the 20th century?
- ☐ England
- ☐ France
- ☐ Germany
- ☐ Japan

3. In snooker what is the score for potting a black?
- ☐ 5
- ☐ 6
- ☐ 7
- ☐ 8

4. Pb is the symbol of which chemical element?
- ☐ Lead
- ☐ Palladium
- ☐ Plutonium
- ☐ Promethium

5. Which term means dying without having made a will?
- ☐ In absentia
- ☐ Intestate
- ☐ Probate
- ☐ Willess

6. Who or what was the Empress of Blandings?

☐ A car
☐ An opera singer
☐ A pig
☐ A vicar

7. How many colours are there in the rainbow?

☐ 7
☐ 8
☐ 9
☐ 10

8. Whom was Madonna desperately seeking in her first feature film?

☐ Amy
☐ Guy Ritchie
☐ Susan
☐ Maradona

9. What type of fruit is dried to produce a sultana?

☐ Apple
☐ Banana
☐ Grape
☐ Sultan

10. What is the name of Sherlock Holmes's housekeeper?

☐ Mrs Baskerville
☐ Mrs Hudson
☐ Mrs Malaprop
☐ Mrs Watson

ANSWERS

1 300. 2 France. 3 7. 4 Lead. 5 Interstate.
6 A pig. 7 7. 8 Susan. 9 Grape. 10 Mrs Hudson.

61

QUIZ 28

1. Where was Glenn Miller flying to when his plane disappeared?
☐ London
☐ Munich
☐ New York
☐ Paris

2. How many squares on a Rubik Cube never move?
☐ 2
☐ 6
☐ 8
☐ 10

3. What did Gloria Gaynor say she would do in 1979?
☐ Be Back
☐ Never Grow Old
☐ Return
☐ Survive

4. What colour is a peridot stone?
☐ Black
☐ Blue
☐ Green
☐ Red

5. In which part of the body is the patella?
☐ Arm
☐ Foot
☐ Head
☐ Knee

6. What is the second letter of the Greek alphabet?

☐ Alpha
☐ Beta
☐ Gamma
☐ Delta

7. What is the nest of an eagle called?

☐ Aigle
☐ Earn
☐ Eyrie
☐ Nestor

8. What type of jewels are traditionally associated with Amsterdam, Holland?

☐ Diamonds
☐ Emerald
☐ Opal
☐ Sapphire

9. What is zoophobia a fear of?

☐ Animals
☐ Cages
☐ People
☐ Zoos

10. Which Irish boy band took their first seven singles to No 1?

☐ Boyzone
☐ New Kids On The Block
☐ One Direction
☐ Westlife

ANSWERS

QUIZ 29

1. Who wrote the mega-selling book *The Da Vinci Code*?
- [ ] Dan Brown
- [ ] David Brown
- [ ] John Grisham
- [ ] Leonardo da Vinci

2. Dr Stephen Hawking wrote a brief history of what?
- [ ] Food
- [ ] Science
- [ ] Space
- [ ] Time

3. How many squares are there on a chess board?
- [ ] 2
- [ ] 32
- [ ] 64
- [ ] 128

4. How many lanes are there in an Olympic swimming pool?
- [ ] 6
- [ ] 7
- [ ] 8
- [ ] 9

5. In which country is Schiphol airport?
- [ ] Belgium
- [ ] France
- [ ] Holland
- [ ] Germany

6. Which event did the first popular greeting card celebrate?

☐ Christmas Day
☐ The Queen's birthday
☐ St George's Day
☐ Valentine's Day

7. What is the home of a beaver called?

☐ Cave
☐ House
☐ Hut
☐ Lodge

8. Of which country was Golda Meir prime minister?

☐ Iraq
☐ Israel
☐ Jordan
☐ Turkey

9. Who wrote of "Season of mists and mellow fruitfulness"?

☐ George Gordon Byron
☐ John Keats
☐ Percy Bysshe Shelley
☐ William Wordsworth

10. Which group recorded the album _Divine Madness_?

☐ The Beat
☐ The Divine Comedy
☐ Madness
☐ The Specials

ANSWERS

1 Dan Brown. 2 Time. 3 64. 4 8. 5 Holland.
6 Valentine's Day. 7 Lodge. 8 Israel. 9 Keats. 10 Madness.

65

QUIZ 30: 80S SOUNDS

1. Which Triangle did Barry Manilow sing about in 1981?
☐ Bermuda
☐ Equilateral
☐ False
☐ Lover's

2. Which "well preserved" group had a hit with "Going Underground"?
☐ The Honeys
☐ The Jam
☐ The Style Council
☐ St Winifred's School Choir

3. What colour was Chris de Burgh's Lady in, in 1986?
☐ Blue
☐ Black
☐ Grey
☐ Red

4. Which band sent a Message in a Bottle?
☐ ABC
☐ Boomtown Rats
☐ Police
☐ Spandau Ballet

5. Where was Billy Joel's Girl in his 1983 Number 1?
☐ Downtown
☐ In Love
☐ Down the chip shop
☐ Uptown

6. Where does Gloria Estefan's Sound Machine come from?

- [ ] Melbourne
- [ ] Merton
- [ ] Mexico
- [ ] Miami

7. What did Jennifer Rush sing about The Power of in 1985?

- [ ] Exercise
- [ ] Love
- [ ] Prayer
- [ ] Us

8. Where did Madness say they were Driving in 1982?

- [ ] In my car
- [ ] Me crazy
- [ ] To Stamford Bridge
- [ ] To the dump

9. What did Cyndi Lauper say Girls wanted to have?

- [ ] Clothes
- [ ] Food
- [ ] Fun
- [ ] TV

10. Where was the Ferry going across on the charity record in 1989?

- [ ] Channel
- [ ] Mersey
- [ ] Road
- [ ] Thames

ANSWERS

1 Bermuda. 2 The Jam. 3 Red. 4 Police. 5 Uptown. 6 Miami. 7 Love. 8 In my car. 9 Fun. 10 Mersey.

67

QUIZ 31

1. How many minutes in two and a half hours?
- ☐ 120
- ☐ 130
- ☐ 140
- ☐ 150

2. Which country is a car from if it has the international registration letters CH?
- ☐ Cuba
- ☐ Hungary
- ☐ Ivory Coast
- ☐ Switzerland

3. What is a segment of garlic called?
- ☐ Bulb
- ☐ Clove
- ☐ Gnarl
- ☐ Slice

4. What is "black gold"?
- ☐ Coal
- ☐ Coffee
- ☐ Oil
- ☐ Paint

5. What word means dry on a bottle of Italian wine?
- ☐ Brut
- ☐ Prosecco
- ☐ Secco
- ☐ Vino

6. According to proverb, how do still waters run?
- ☐ Blue
- ☐ Cold
- ☐ Deep
- ☐ Dry

7. What is hippophobia a fear of?
- ☐ Camels
- ☐ Cows
- ☐ Hippopotamuses
- ☐ Horses

8. What type of food is a bloomer?
- ☐ Bread
- ☐ Edible flower
- ☐ Fruit
- ☐ Vegetable

9. What colour do you get if you mix red and yellow?
- ☐ Blue
- ☐ Green
- ☐ Orange
- ☐ White

10. How many sides has a rhombus?
- ☐ 4
- ☐ 5
- ☐ 8
- ☐ 9

ANSWERS

QUIZ 32

1. Born Arthur Jefferson in 1890, what was this comic better known as?
- [ ] Charlie Chaplin
- [ ] Oliver Hardy
- [ ] Buster Keaton
- [ ] Stan Laurel

2. Who partnered Robbie Williams on the hit single "Kids"?
- [ ] Dannii Minogue
- [ ] Kylie Minogue
- [ ] Geri Halliwell
- [ ] Jonathan Wilkes

3. Titan is a moon of which planet?
- [ ] Mercury
- [ ] Pluto
- [ ] Saturn
- [ ] Uranus

4. Who is the only singer to have No 1 hits in the 50s, 60s, 70s, 80s and 90s?
- [ ] David Bowie
- [ ] Tom Jones
- [ ] Cliff Richard
- [ ] Frank Sinatra

5. How many furlongs in a mile?
- [ ] 4
- [ ] 6
- [ ] 8
- [ ] 12

6. Which annual race was first held in 1829?

☐ The Derby
☐ London Marathon
☐ Oxford and Cambridge boat race
☐ Tour de France

7. Which is the odd one out?

☐ Garibaldi
☐ Ginger Nut
☐ Mars
☐ Nice

8. What did Siam change its name to?

☐ Phillipines
☐ Malaysia
☐ Singapore
☐ Thailand

9.If a triangle has internal angles of 58 and 77 degrees, what is the third internal angle?

☐ 35
☐ 45
☐ 55
☐ 65

10. Which king of England abdicated and was succeeded by his younger brother?

☐ Edward V
☐ Edward VI
☐ Edward VII
☐ Edward VIII

ANSWERS

1 Stan Laurel. 2 Kylie Minogue. 3 Saturn. 4 Cliff Richard. 5 8. 6 Oxford/Cambridge boat race. 7 Mars (the others are biscuits). 8 Thailand. 9 45. 10 Edward VIII.

QUIZ 33

1. Which fictional bear is named after a London station?
☐ Euston
☐ King Cross
☐ Liverpool
☐ Paddington

2. What is the largest state of the USA?
☐ Alaska
☐ Montana
☐ New York
☐ Texas

3. In which month is the shortest day?
☐ November
☐ December
☐ January
☐ February

4. In which sport is the Thomas Cup awarded?
☐ Badminton
☐ Cricket
☐ Darts
☐ Tennis

5. In which year were women first allowed to take degrees at British universities?
☐ 1868
☐ 1878
☐ 1908
☐ 1918

6. Which bird is associated with Lundy Island?

- [ ] Eagle
- [ ] Lund
- [ ] Puffin
- [ ] Tern

7. In the solar system which is the third planet from the sun?

- [ ] Earth
- [ ] Pluto
- [ ] Saturn
- [ ] Uranus

8. According to proverb, a little what is a dangerous thing?

- [ ] Greed
- [ ] Knowledge
- [ ] Learning
- [ ] Money

9. What would you be playing if you were talking about spares and strikes?

- [ ] Bowling
- [ ] Bowls
- [ ] Curling
- [ ] Matchbox collecting

10. What was the name of Barnum's famous giant elephant?

- [ ] Barnum
- [ ] Dumbo
- [ ] Ellie
- [ ] Jumbo

ANSWERS

1 Paddington. 2 Alaska. 3 December. 4 Badminton. 5 1878. 6 Puffin.
7 Earth. 8 Knowledge. 9 Bowling. 10 Jumbo.

73

QUIZ 34: GEOGRAPHY

1. The Bay of Biscay lies directly to the north of which country?
☐ France
☐ Morocco
☐ Portugal
☐ Spain

2. Which Gulf lies between Iran and Saudi Arabia?
☐ Gulf of Aden
☐ Gulf of Bothnia
☐ Gulf of Oman
☐ Persian Gulf

3. Brittany is part of which country?
☐ Belgium
☐ France
☐ Great Britain
☐ Wales

4. In which country is Shanghai?
☐ China
☐ Japan
☐ Malaysia
☐ Singapore

5. In which country is Zurich?
☐ Austria
☐ Germany
☐ Hungary
☐ Switzerland

6. In which country is the holiday destination of Bali?

☐ Australia
☐ India
☐ Indonesia
☐ Philippines

7. Which group of islands does Gran Canaria belong to?

☐ Aleutian Islands
☐ Balearic Islands
☐ Canary Islands
☐ Cook Islands

8. Where would you be if you had climbed Mount Olympus?

☐ Albania
☐ Greece
☐ Turkey
☐ USA

9. In which US state is Orlando?

☐ California
☐ Florida
☐ Rhode Island
☐ Texas

10. Which Falls are on the Canadian/US border?

☐ Angel
☐ Iguazu
☐ Niagara
☐ Victoria

ANSWERS

6 Indonesia. 7 Canary Islands. 8 Greece. 9 Florida. 10 Niagara.
1 Spain. 2 Persian Gulf. 3 France. 4 China. 5 Switzerland.

75

QUIZ 35

1. How many sheets of paper are there in a ream?
- ☐ 250
- ☐ 500
- ☐ 750
- ☐ 1,000

2. Which country are Qantas airlines from?
- ☐ Australia
- ☐ Egypt
- ☐ Qatar
- ☐ United Arab Emirates

3. In rhyming slang what is Barnet Fair?
- ☐ Tony Blair
- ☐ Chair
- ☐ Flared trousers
- ☐ Hair

4. How is Declan McManus better known?
- ☐ Elvis Costelloe
- ☐ Shane MacGowan
- ☐ Elvis Presley
- ☐ Van Morrison

5. What animal is shown in the painting "The Monarch of the Glen"?
- ☐ A black and white cow
- ☐ A black deer stag
- ☐ A Man
- ☐ A red deer stag

6. What is the first name of Polish film director Polanski?

☐ Artur
☐ Heinrich
☐ John
☐ Roman

7. What colour is saffron?

☐ Brown
☐ Green
☐ White
☐ Yellow

8. What was Al short for in Al Capone's name?

☐ Alamo
☐ Alfred
☐ Alphonse
☐ Antonio

9. How many sides has a trapezium?

☐ 3
☐ 4
☐ 7
☐ 9

10. Which metal is an alloy of copper and zinc?

☐ Aluminium
☐ Brass
☐ Bronze
☐ Tin

ANSWERS

5 A red deer stag. 6 Roman. 7 Yellow. 8 Alphonse. 9 4. 10 Brass.
1 500. 2 Australia. 3 Hair. 4 Elvis Costelloe.

77

QUIZ 36

1. Which country did Prime Minister Bhutto rule?
- [ ] India
- [ ] Malaysia
- [ ] Pakistan
- [ ] Sri Lanka

2. What is the capital of Sweden?
- [ ] Copenhagen
- [ ] Gothenburg
- [ ] Malmo
- [ ] Stockholm

3. What is Roget's word book known as?
- [ ] Dictionary
- [ ] Glossary
- [ ] Index
- [ ] Thesaurus

4. Which David told his life story in *The Moon's a Balloon*?
- [ ] Beckham
- [ ] Bowie
- [ ] Davies
- [ ] Niven

5. Rocks are broken down by the elements by what gradual process?
- [ ] Compacting
- [ ] Erosion
- [ ] Gravity
- [ ] Weathering

6. Which tenor took the title role in *The Great Caruso*?

☐ Jose Carreras
☐ Placido Domingo
☐ Mario Lanza
☐ Luciano Pavarotti

7. The word lupine relates to which animals?

☐ Dogs
☐ Lions
☐ Rats
☐ Wolves

8. In which country is the volcano Popocatépetl?

☐ Chile
☐ Guatemala
☐ Mexico
☐ Uruguay

9. Which element is found in bones, shells and teeth?

☐ Cadmium
☐ Calcium
☐ Californium
☐ Carbon

10. What does the French word *vacances* mean?

☐ Hello
☐ Goodbye
☐ Holiday
☐ Vaccination

ANSWERS

1 Pakistan. 2 Stockholm. 3 Thesaurus. 4 Niven. 5 Weathering. 6. Mario Lanza. 7 Wolves. 8 Mexico. 9 Calcium. 10 Holiday.

79

QUIZ 37

1. Which sport awards the Harmsworth Trophy?
☐ BMX
☐ Moto-cross
☐ Power boat racing
☐ Rugby

2. What is the Paris underground referred to as?
☐ Metro
☐ Subway
☐ The Tube
☐ L'underground

3. What is the word for a group of hounds?
☐ Deck
☐ Herd
☐ Litter
☐ Pack

4. Which New England poet said he had "miles to go before I sleep"?
☐ Robert Frost
☐ Edgar Allen Poe
☐ Walt Whitman
☐ William Wordsworth

5. Which work does Anitra's Dance come from?
☐ Dvorak's New World Symphony
☐ Grieg's Peer Gynt
☐ Grieg's Symphonic Dances
☐ Sibelius's Seven Songs

6. Which planet does Superman come from?

☐ Discworld
☐ Krypton
☐ Mobius
☐ Vulcan

7. What is the zodiac sign of the Crab?

☐ Aries
☐ Cancer
☐ Leo
☐ Virgo

8. In golf what is the term for two over par?

☐ Bogey
☐ Double-bogey
☐ Eagle
☐ Two-over

9. What were followers of John Wycliffe called?

☐ Dullards
☐ Fops
☐ Lollards
☐ Whigs

10. Who said – though not in English – "I think therefore I am"?

☐ René Descartes
☐ Immanuel Kant
☐ John Locke
☐ Baruch Spinoza

ANSWERS

1 Power boat racing. 2 Metro. 3 Pack. 4 Robert Frost. 5 Peer Gynt. 6 Krypton. 7 Cancer. 8 Double-bogey. 9 Lollards. 10 René Descartes.

81

QUIZ 38: INVENTIONS

1. What was invented by Lazlo and Georg Biro?

☐ Ball-point pen
☐ Bicycle
☐ Safety razor
☐ Telescope

2. What nationality was motor vehicle pioneer Gottlieb Daimler?

☐ Austrian
☐ English
☐ German
☐ Polish

3. What did John Logie Baird invent?

☐ Internal combustion engine
☐ Radio
☐ Television
☐ Wifi

4. Which method of food preservation did Clarence Birdseye invent?

☐ Freezing
☐ Smoking
☐ Tinned goods
☐ Vacuum packing

5. What powered James Watt's engine in 1765?

☐ Elastic
☐ Oil
☐ Petrol
☐ Steam

6. Something was special about the fabric Charles Macintosh invented? Was it...

☐ Coloured
☐ Elastic
☐ Unrippable
☐ Waterproof

7. Which tourists' essential was invented by American Express?

☐ Credit card
☐ Passport
☐ Suitcase
☐ Travellers cheque

8. Which food was developed by Will Keith Kellogg in 1898?

☐ Cheerios
☐ Cornflakes
☐ Rice Krispies
☐ Weetabix

9. For whom did Louis Braille develop his writing system?

☐ The blind
☐ The deaf
☐ The poor
☐ People with arthritis

10. Which communication system is Alexander Graham Bell famous for?

☐ Morse code
☐ Semaphore
☐ Telephone
☐ Walkie-talkie

QUIZ 39

1. Catherine Parr survived which royal husband?
- ☐ Prince Charles
- ☐ Edward VII
- ☐ Henry V
- ☐ Henry VIII

2. What is meant by the Latin phrase caveat emptor?
- ☐ Buyer beware
- ☐ Check your pockets
- ☐ Don't sell things
- ☐ Empty your pockets

3. What spirit is made from fermented sugar cane?
- ☐ Gin
- ☐ Rum
- ☐ Vodka
- ☐ Whisky

4. What paper is used to test acid and alkali?
- ☐ Acid paper
- ☐ Alkali paper
- ☐ Litmus paper
- ☐ Sugar paper

5. Which special day follows Shrove Tuesday?
- ☐ Ash Wednesday
- ☐ Leftover Wednesday
- ☐ Pancake Wednesday
- ☐ Passover Wednesday

6. How is the UK golfing term albatross known in America?

☐ Double bogey
☐ Double eagle
☐ Double top
☐ Nearly-hole-in-one

7. What name is adopted by Don Diego de la Vega?

☐ Diego Maradona
☐ Don Seagal
☐ Zarathustra
☐ Zorro

8. What were the first three Eddystone lighthouses lit by?

☐ Batteries
☐ Candles
☐ Electricity
☐ Fire

9. What is a young hare called?

☐ Calf
☐ Chick
☐ Leveret
☐ Pup

10. Which nuts are used to make marzipan?

☐ Almonds
☐ Cashews
☐ Hazelnuts
☐ Peanuts

ANSWERS

1 Henry VIII. 2 Buyer beware. 3 Rum. 4 Litmus. 5 Ash Wednesday. 6 Double eagle. 7 Zorro. 8 Candles. 9 Leveret. 10 Almonds.

QUIZ 40

1. What is the national flower of Austria?
- ☐ Crocus
- ☐ Edelweiss
- ☐ Rose
- ☐ Tulip

2. Which monarch is credited with writing "Greensleeves"?
- ☐ Edward VII
- ☐ Henry IV
- ☐ Henry V
- ☐ Henry VIII

3. In which month is St Patrick's Day?
- ☐ February
- ☐ March
- ☐ April
- ☐ May

4. What is dried in an oast house?
- ☐ Clothes
- ☐ Grain
- ☐ Hops
- ☐ Rice

5. What is a young kangaroo called?
- ☐ Cub
- ☐ Joey
- ☐ Lassie
- ☐ Skippy

6. Name the first British winner of the Tour de France?
- [ ] Chris Boardman
- [ ] Mark Cavendish
- [ ] Chris Froome
- [ ] Bradley Wiggins

7. In which city did the Barbican arts centre open?
- [ ] London
- [ ] Munich
- [ ] New York
- [ ] Paris

8. In snooker, how many points are scored by potting the yellow ball?
- [ ] 2
- [ ] 5
- [ ] 6
- [ ] 7

9. Cu is the symbol of which chemical element?
- [ ] Carbon
- [ ] Chromium
- [ ] Cobalt
- [ ] Copper

10. In which county is Land's End?
- [ ] Avon
- [ ] Cornwall
- [ ] Devon
- [ ] Somerset

ANSWERS

1 Edelweiss. 2 Henry VIII. 3 March. 4 Hops. 5 Joey. 6 Bradley Wiggins. 7 London. 8 2. 9 Copper. 10 Cornwall.

87

QUIZ 41

1. What is the medical name for dizziness due to heights?

☐ Disequilibrium
☐ Dizzyness
☐ Varicella
☐ Vertigo

2. On a map, what are lines called that join places of equal height above sea level?

☐ Contour lines
☐ Grid
☐ Key
☐ Scale

3. How many pints in three quarts?

☐ 2
☐ 4
☐ 6
☐ 8

4. From which plant is linen obtained?

☐ Cotton
☐ Fern
☐ Flax
☐ Fluxroot

5. What size was Tim in *A Christmas Carol*?

☐ Big
☐ Little
☐ Small
☐ Tiny

6. What did Al Capone have on his face that gave him his nickname?

- ☐ Freckles
- ☐ Glasses
- ☐ Scar
- ☐ Warts

7. In nursery rhyme, where did Mary's little lamb follow her to?

- ☐ Home
- ☐ Nursery
- ☐ School
- ☐ Work

8. What do volleyball players hit the ball with?

- ☐ Feet
- ☐ Hands
- ☐ Head
- ☐ Knees

9. According to the proverb, what does the devil make work for?

- ☐ Details
- ☐ Idle hands
- ☐ Lazy people
- ☐ Pulling up socks

10. What type of food is a pomelo?

- ☐ Cake
- ☐ Fruit
- ☐ Seed
- ☐ Vegetable

ANSWERS

1 Vertigo. 2 Contour lines. 3 6. 4 Flax. 5 Tiny. 6 Scar. 7 School. 8 Hands. 9 Idle hands. 10 Fruit.

89

QUIZ 42: ARTISTS

1. Which John painted "The Hay Wain"?

☐ Constable
☐ Delacroix
☐ Gainsborough
☐ Turner

2. What was the surname of outrageous artist Salvador?

☐ Dada
☐ Dali
☐ Darling
☐ Warhol

3. What was the first name of Impressionist painter Cézanne?

☐ Arthur
☐ Paul
☐ Pierre
☐ Pavel

4. Which parts of the Venus de Milo are missing?

☐ Arms
☐ Ears
☐ Eyes
☐ Feet

5. Which animals is George Stubbs famous for painting?

☐ Cats
☐ Deer
☐ Horses
☐ Sheep

6. What was the first name of pop artist Warhol?

☐ Andy
☐ Andrij
☐ Mike
☐ Paolo

7. What was the nationality of Rembrandt?

☐ British
☐ Dutch
☐ French
☐ Italian

8. What is the first name of pop artist Hockney?

☐ Art
☐ David
☐ Peter
☐ Simon

9. What was the nationality of portrait painter Millais?

☐ Belgian
☐ English
☐ French
☐ Irish

10. Which English artist is famous for his matchstalk men pictures?

☐ Peter Blake
☐ Antony Gormley
☐ Richard Long
☐ L.S. Lowry

QUIZ 43

1. How many packs of cards are needed for a game of Canasta?
- [ ] 1
- [ ] 2
- [ ] 3
- [ ] 4

2. Which character did Harrison Ford play in Star Wars?
- [ ] Jabba
- [ ] Jar Jar
- [ ] Luke Skywalker
- [ ] Han Solo

3. What is a sabot?
- [ ] Car
- [ ] Clog
- [ ] Cheese
- [ ] Fruit

4. Bill Gates founded which computer corporation?
- [ ] Apple
- [ ] Dell
- [ ] IBM
- [ ] Microsoft

5. Whom did Sirhan Sirhan assassinate?
- [ ] John F. Kennedy
- [ ] Robert Kennedy
- [ ] Teddy Kennedy
- [ ] Lee Harvey Oswald

6. What is ruled by the House of Grimaldi?

- ☐ Italy
- ☐ Monaco
- ☐ The Senate
- ☐ Vatican City

7. Who jumped off the Tallahatchee Bridge?

- ☐ Bobbie Gentry
- ☐ Bobbi Lee
- ☐ Billy Joe McAllister
- ☐ Becky Thompson

8. What type of food is consommé?

- ☐ Bread
- ☐ Cheese
- ☐ Dessert
- ☐ Soup

9. How is Norma Jean Baker better known?

- ☐ Adele
- ☐ Elizabeth Taylor
- ☐ Lady GaGa
- ☐ Marilyn Monroe

10. What colour features in the title of George Gershwin's Rhapsody?

- ☐ Blue
- ☐ Green
- ☐ Red
- ☐ Yellow

ANSWERS

1 2 Han Solo. 3 Clog. 4 Microsoft. 5 Robert Kennedy. 6 Monaco. 7 Billy Joe McAllister. 8 Soup. 9 Marilyn Monroe. 10 Blue

93

QUIZ 44

1. Which extra title was given to Catherine II of Russia?
☐ Of Aragon
☐ The Great
☐ The Impaler
☐ Parr

2. Which country is a car from if it has the international registration letter H?
☐ England
☐ Holland
☐ Hungary
☐ Switzerland

3. Zn is the symbol of which chemical element?
☐ Zebronium
☐ Zeponium
☐ Zinc
☐ Zirconium

4. According to proverb, one man's meat is another man's what?
☐ Cheese
☐ Dinner
☐ Poison
☐ Vegetable

5.What is the capital of Afghanistan?
☐ Kabul
☐ Kandahar
☐ Peshawar
☐ Tashkent

6. How many yards in a mile?

☐ 960
☐ 1,280
☐ 1,540
☐ 1,760

7. Which US playwright wrote *The Price*?

☐ James Dougherty
☐ D H Lawrence
☐ W Somerset Maughm
☐ Arthur Miller

8. What colour pottery is Josiah Wedgwood noted for?

☐ Black
☐ Blue
☐ White
☐ Yellow

9. In nursery rhyme, what did Little Jack Horner pull out of a pie?

☐ Apple
☐ Banana
☐ Magpies
☐ Plum

10. According to proverb, what is a change as good as?

☐ Another change
☐ A long holiday
☐ A new job
☐ A rest

ANSWERS

1 The Great. 2 Hungary. 3 Zinc. 4 Poison. 5 Kabul. 6 1,760. 7 Arthur Miller. 8 Blue. 9 Plum. 10 A rest.

95

QUIZ 45

1. Which country is a car from if it has the international registration letter J?
- [ ] Jamaica
- [ ] Japan
- [ ] Jordan
- [ ] Switzerland

2. Which Oscar said, "I have nothing to declare except my genius."
- [ ] Coward
- [ ] Ghandi
- [ ] Hammerstein
- [ ] Wilde

3. Bovine relates to which kind of animals?
- [ ] Cats
- [ ] Cows
- [ ] Dogs
- [ ] Sheep

4. What is the chief ingredient in the production of glass?
- [ ] Metal
- [ ] Sand
- [ ] Stone
- [ ] Water

5. How many sides in three rectangles?
- [ ] 9
- [ ] 10
- [ ] 11
- [ ] 12

6. What sort of Attraction was there between Michael Douglas and Glenn Close?

- [ ] Fatal
- [ ] Killer
- [ ] Naughty
- [ ] Suicidal

7. What type of pre-wedding party is for women only?

- [ ] Batchelor
- [ ] Hen
- [ ] Stag
- [ ] Shower

8. What are pipistrelles?

- [ ] Bats
- [ ] Cats
- [ ] Rats
- [ ] Statues

9. Which nickname did saxophonist Julian Adderley acquire?

- [ ] Bird
- [ ] Cannonball
- [ ] Jellyroll
- [ ] Tiger

10. Who wrote *Lord Jim*?

- [ ] Chinua Achebe
- [ ] Joseph Conrad
- [ ] Henry James
- [ ] D.H. Lawrence

ANSWERS

1 Japan. 2 Wilde. 3 Cowa. 4 Sand. 5 12. 6 Fatal. 7 Hen. 8 Bats. 9 Cannonball. 10 Joseph Conrad.

97

QUIZ 46: 90S SOUNDS

1. Where was Love in the 1994 hit by Wet Wet Wet?

☐ All Around
☐ Everywhere
☐ Nowhere
☐ Out to Lunch

2. Who had a hit in 1992 with "I Will Always Love You", the theme from *The Bodyguard*?

☐ Toni Braxton
☐ Mariah Carey
☐ Whitney Houston
☐ Luther Vandross

3. Which part of East London sang "Stay Another Day" in 1994?

☐ East 17
☐ East Ham
☐ Hackney Crew
☐ NKOTB

4. Which 50-plus female took "Believe" to the top of the charts?

☐ Cher
☐ Cyndi Lauper
☐ Tina Turner
☐ Bonnie Tyler

5. Who wore Crocodile Shoes in 1994?

☐ Elvis Costelloe
☐ Gary Holdon
☐ Jimmy Nail
☐ Shakin Stevens

6. Who joined George Michael on "Don't Let the Sun Go Down on Me"?

- [ ] Boy George
- [ ] Mick Hucknall
- [ ] Elton John
- [ ] Andrew Ridgeley

7. "Everything I Do (I Do It for You)" came from a film about which hero?

- [ ] Robin Hood
- [ ] The Man in the Iron Mask
- [ ] Superman
- [ ] The Three Musketeers

8. Which Streets did Bruce Springsteen sing about in 1994?

- [ ] Mean
- [ ] Happy
- [ ] New York
- [ ] Philadelphia

9. What nationality is Björk?

- [ ] Danish
- [ ] Finnish
- [ ] Icelandic
- [ ] Swedish

10. Which Ebenezer was in the tile of the song by the Shamen?

- [ ] Bad
- [ ] "E"
- [ ] Goode
- [ ] Scrooge

ANSWERS

1 All Around. 2 Whitney Houston. 3 East 17. 4 Cher. 5 Jimmy Nail. 6 Elton John. 7 Robin Hood. 8 Philadelphia. 9 Icelandic. 10 Goode.

99

QUIZ 47

1. What city is the capital of Kuwait?
☐ Al Ahmadi
☐ Basrah
☐ Kuwait City
☐ Kuwaitown

2. Who wrote the poem "Sea Fever"?
☐ Robert Bridges
☐ Walter de la Mare
☐ John Ireland
☐ John Masefield

3. In the children's party game, what is passed around and unwrapped?
☐ Cake
☐ Parcel
☐ Pinata
☐ Shoes

4. In which month is Halloween?
☐ October
☐ November
☐ December
☐ January

5. On what part of your body would you wear a homburg?
☐ Feet
☐ Hands
☐ Head
☐ Legs

6. In which city did the hamburger originate?

☐ Frankfurt
☐ Hamburg
☐ New York
☐ Paris

7. Who recorded the album *I Am... Sasha Fierce*?

☐ Alicia Keys
☐ Beyoncé
☐ Rihanna
☐ Kelly Rowland

8. What would you find in an arboretum?

☐ Animals
☐ Flowers
☐ Gravestones
☐ Trees

9. What type of animal is a natterjack?

☐ Bird
☐ Dog
☐ Frog
☐ Toad

10. What superhero can Peter Parker turn into?

☐ Batman
☐ Green Goblin
☐ Spider-man
☐ Superman

ANSWERS

1 Kuwait City. 2 John Masefield. 3 Parcel. 4 October. 5 Head. 6 Hamburg. 7 Beyoncé. 8 Trees. 9 Toad. 10 Spider-man.

QUIZ 48

1. Which English queen never married?
- [ ] Anne
- [ ] Elizabeth I
- [ ] Elizabeth II
- [ ] Victoria

2. What does the word hirsute mean?
- [ ] Angry
- [ ] Hairy
- [ ] Naughty
- [ ] Silly

3. Who wrote *Little Men*?
- [ ] Louisa May Alcott
- [ ] Amos Bronson Alcott
- [ ] Nathaniel Hawthorne
- [ ] Ralph Waldo Emerson

4. In feet how wide is a hockey goal?
- [ ] 9
- [ ] 10
- [ ] 11
- [ ] 12

5. Which major river flows through New Orleans?
- [ ] Amazon
- [ ] Mississippi
- [ ] Missouri
- [ ] St Lawrence

6. Whose last words were, "Thank God I have done my duty"?
- [ ] Napoleon Bonaparte
- [ ] Winston Churchill
- [ ] Horatio Nelson
- [ ] Arthur Wellesley

7. Which country did General Franco rule?
- [ ] France
- [ ] Germany
- [ ] Portugal
- [ ] Spain

8. Where is the Sea of Showers?
- [ ] Australia
- [ ] Brazil
- [ ] The Moon
- [ ] USA/Canada border

9. Which game is connected with Boris Schapiro?
- [ ] Badminton
- [ ] Bridge
- [ ] Poker
- [ ] Tennis

10. What kind of animal features in the book *Watership Down*?
- [ ] Cow
- [ ] Cat
- [ ] Dog
- [ ] Rabbit

———————————————————————— ANSWERS

1 Elizabeth 2 Hairy 3 Louisa May Alcott 4 12, 5 Mississippi. 6 Horatio Nelson. 7 Spain. 8 The Moon. 9 Bridge. 10 Rabbit.

103

QUIZ 49

1. Who had a hit with "Bridge Over Troubled Water"?
- [ ] Donovan
- [ ] The Mamas & the Papas
- [ ] Simon & Garfunkel
- [ ] Cat Stevens

2. In nursery rhyme, during which season did the Queen of Hearts make the tarts?
- [ ] Spring
- [ ] Summer
- [ ] Autumn
- [ ] Winter

3. What life-threatening thing appeared in London for the last time in 1962?
- [ ] Flood
- [ ] Godzilla
- [ ] Smog
- [ ] Typhoid

4. What is the name of the disc used in ice hockey?
- [ ] Ball
- [ ] Duck
- [ ] Discus
- [ ] Puck

5. What vehicles race in the Indianapolis 500?
- [ ] Bicycles
- [ ] Cars
- [ ] Tractors
- [ ] Trucks

6. What colour did all lupins used to be?

- [ ] Black
- [ ] Blue
- [ ] Green
- [ ] Red

7. What is the wife of an Earl called?

- [ ] Countess
- [ ] Dutchess
- [ ] Earlette
- [ ] Shearle

8. In which city is Orly airport?

- [ ] Orlando
- [ ] Oakland
- [ ] Orléans
- [ ] Paris

9. The Kentucky Derby is a horse race in which country?

- [ ] Australia
- [ ] South Africa
- [ ] UK
- [ ] USA

10. In rhyming slang what is a Joanna?

- [ ] Car
- [ ] Piano
- [ ] Radio
- [ ] Telesivion

ANSWERS

1 Simon & Garfunkel. 2 Summer. 3 Smog. 4 Puck. 5 Cars. 6 Blue. 7 Countess. 8 Paris. 9 USA. 10 Piano.

105

QUIZ 50: FOOD & DRINK

1. What type of drink is Darjeeling?

- [ ] Alcohol
- [ ] Coffee
- [ ] Hot chocolate
- [ ] Tea

2. What colour is the flesh of an avocado?

- [ ] Blue
- [ ] Green
- [ ] Red
- [ ] White

3. If a drink was served "on the rocks", what would it have in the glass?

- [ ] Ice
- [ ] Lemon
- [ ] Rocks
- [ ] Water

4. What colour is paprika?

- [ ] Blue
- [ ] Green
- [ ] Red
- [ ] White

5. What is the main ingredient of a traditional fondue?

- [ ] Bread
- [ ] Butter
- [ ] Cheese
- [ ] Chocolate

6. Which food accompaniment is Dijon famous for?

- ☐ Brown sauce
- ☐ Ketchup
- ☐ Mayonnaise
- ☐ Mustard

7. What is the fruit flavour of Cointreau?

- ☐ Apple
- ☐ Banana
- ☐ Lemon
- ☐ Orange

8. What type of vegetable is a Maris Piper?

- ☐ Cabbage
- ☐ Carrot
- ☐ Pea
- ☐ Potato

9. Which county does Wensleydale cheese traditionally come from?

- ☐ Cornwall
- ☐ Devon
- ☐ Somerset
- ☐ Yorkshire

10. What colour is crème de menthe?

- ☐ Blue
- ☐ Clear
- ☐ Green
- ☐ White

ANSWERS

1 Tea. 2 Green 4. 3 Ice. 4 Red. 5 Cheese. 6 Mustard. 7 Orange. 8 Potatoe. 9 Yorkshire. 10 Green.

107

QUIZ 51

1. Which season does the word vernal relate to?

☐ Winter
☐ Spring
☐ Summer
☐ Autumn

2. On which island are most lemurs found?

☐ Easter Island
☐ Madagascar
☐ Mauritius
☐ Seychelles

3. Who wrote the Aldwych farces, including *Rookery Nook*?

☐ Robertson Hare
☐ Ralph Lynn
☐ Ben Travers
☐ Tom Wall

4. In rhyming slang what is dog and bone?

☐ Babysitter
☐ Butcher's shop
☐ Dog
☐ Telephone

5. What was Farrokh Bulsara better known as?

☐ Elton John
☐ Tom Jones
☐ Freddie Mercury
☐ Cliff Richard

6. What colour is associated with an Oxford or Cambridge sports award?

☐ Black
☐ Blue
☐ Brown
☐ Gold

7. In tennis, what name is given to a serve that cannot be returned?

☐ Ace
☐ Deuce
☐ Love
☐ One-way serve

8. What was the first name of Burgess, the famous spy?

☐ Anthony
☐ Donald
☐ Guy
☐ Kim

9. In which street is the Bank of England?

☐ Bank
☐ Monument Street
☐ Moorgate
☐ Threadneedle Street

10. What is another name for the creature the axolotl?

☐ Dinosaur
☐ Lizard
☐ Newt
☐ Salamander

ANSWERS

1 Spring, 2 Madagascar, 3 Ben Travers, 4 Telephone, 5 Freddie Mercury, 6 Blue, 7 Ace, 8 Guy, 9 Threadneedle Street, 10 (Mexican) Salamander.

109

QUIZ 52

1. How many minutes in half a day?
- [ ] 360
- [ ] 480
- [ ] 560
- [ ] 720

2. Who wrote "Don't Let's be Beastly to the Germans"?
- [ ] Noel Coward
- [ ] Winston Churchill
- [ ] Oscar Hammerstein II
- [ ] Gertrude Lawrence

3. Ag is the symbol of which chemical element?
- [ ] Gold
- [ ] Magnesium
- [ ] Manganese
- [ ] Silver

4. Who was lead singer with Them?
- [ ] Jackson Browne
- [ ] Eric Clapton
- [ ] Van Morrison
- [ ] Steve Winwood

5. Avian relates to which kind of creatures?
- [ ] Birds
- [ ] Cats
- [ ] Dogs
- [ ] Sheep

6. Which of the following was written first by Olivia Manning?

☐ The Balkan Trilogy
☐ The Levant Trilogy
☐ The New York Trilogy
☐ The Scunthorpe Trilogy

7. What was the name of the boy in *The Jungle Book*?

☐ Doolittle
☐ Baloo
☐ Mowgli
☐ Kaspar Hauser

8. What game is played at St Andrews?

☐ Curling
☐ Darts
☐ Football
☐ Golf

9. What is the nickname of the New Zealand rugby team?

☐ All blacks
☐ Harlequins
☐ Kiwis
☐ Springboks

10. How much does it cost to buy a station on a British Monopoly board?

☐ £50
☐ £100
☐ £150
☐ £200

————————————————————————— ANSWERS

1 720. 2 Noel Coward. 3 Silver. 4 Van Morrison of Kent. 5 Birds. 6 The Balkan Trilogy 7 Mowgli. 8 Golf. 9 All Blacks. 10 £200.

111

QUIZ 53

1. How many strings are there on a Spanish guitar?
- ☐ 4
- ☐ 6
- ☐ 8
- ☐ 12

2. How did the notorious witchfinder Matthew Hopkins die?
- ☐ Burned at the stake
- ☐ Committed suicide
- ☐ Hanged as a wizard
- ☐ Tuberculosis

3. What type of hat was worn by Sherlock Holmes?
- ☐ Bowler
- ☐ Deerstalker
- ☐ Flat cap
- ☐ Panama

4. What was the "Flying Scotsman"?
- ☐ Airplane
- ☐ Motorbike
- ☐ Person
- ☐ Train

5. What type of food is a profiterole?
- ☐ Cheese
- ☐ Dessert
- ☐ Fruit
- ☐ Starter

6. Which Russian ruler was known as "the Terrible"?

- [ ] Ivan
- [ ] Lenin
- [ ] Trotsky
- [ ] Vlad

7. What was the surname of landscape gardener Capability?

- [ ] Brown
- [ ] Green
- [ ] Lawn
- [ ] Trunk

8. In mythology what is Neptune the god of?

- [ ] Ghosts
- [ ] People
- [ ] The Sea
- [ ] Wine

9. In which musical does the song "Somewhere" appear?

- [ ] Paint Your Wagon
- [ ] The Sound of Music
- [ ] West Side Story
- [ ] Wonderful Town

10. Which dance goes, one-two-three-hop?

- [ ] Can can
- [ ] Congo
- [ ] Polka
- [ ] Tarantella

ANSWERS

9 West Side Story. 10 Polka.

1 6. 2 Tuberculosis. 3 Deerstalker. 4 Train. 5 Dessert. 6 Ivan. 7 Brown. 8 The Sea.

Quiz 54: Pop charts

1. Whose first chart success was "Your Song"?
- [ ] David Bowie
- [ ] Elton John
- [ ] Cliff Richard
- [ ] Tommy Steele

2. Which David charted with both Bing Crosby and Mick Jagger?
- [ ] Bowie
- [ ] Davies
- [ ] Cameron
- [ ] Duchovny

3. What is Paul McCartney's middle name?
- [ ] George
- [ ] John
- [ ] Paul
- [ ] Ringo

4. Which Rod has had over 50 chart hits?
- [ ] Hull
- [ ] Jones
- [ ] Stewart
- [ ] Taylor

5. Dido's song "Thank You" was sampled by which rapper on his song "Stan"?
- [ ] Biggie Smalls
- [ ] Eminem
- [ ] Jay-Z
- [ ] Tupac

6. Where in London did the Kinks watch the Sunset?

☐ Hackney
☐ Oxford Street
☐ Paddington
☐ Waterloo

7. Who were Alone in the charts, 30 years after their first hit?

☐ Abba
☐ Bee Gees
☐ ELO
☐ Queen

8. Which New Kids had seven singles in the charts in 1990?

☐ Backstreet
☐ 'N Sync
☐ On The Block
☐ Westlife

9. "Song for Whoever" was the first hit for which Beautiful group?

☐ Beautiful Housemartins
☐ Beautiful North
☐ Beautiful People
☐ Beautiful South

10. In which decade did charts start to be compiled in the UK?

☐ 1930s
☐ 1940s
☐ 1950s
☐ 1960s

1 Elton John. 2 Bowie. 3 Paul. 4 Stewart. 5 Eminem. 6 Waterloo. 7 Bee Gees. 8 On The Block. 9 Beautiful South. 10 1950s.

QUIZ 55

1. What is the seventh commandment?
- [ ] Thou shalt not commit adultery
- [ ] Thou shalt have no other gods before me
- [ ] Thou shalt not kill
- [ ] Thou shalt not steal

2. What sport takes place in a velodrome?
- [ ] Bungee jumping
- [ ] Cycling
- [ ] Flying
- [ ] Gymnastics

3. In which card game do you "peg out"?
- [ ] Canasta
- [ ] Cribbage
- [ ] Pegger
- [ ] Poker

4. Which bingo number is clickety click?
- [ ] 11
- [ ] 22
- [ ] 66
- [ ] 88

5. What colour is ebony?
- [ ] Blue
- [ ] Black
- [ ] Brown
- [ ] White

6. What do you have at the bottom of a colander?

☐ Holes
☐ Metal
☐ Spikes
☐ Wood

7. What colour are French post boxes?

☐ Blue
☐ Green
☐ Red
☐ Yellow

8. Whose motto is "Nation shall speak unto nation"?

☐ The BBC
☐ The European Union
☐ The United Nations
☐ The United States of America

9. What sort of Circle do conjurers join?

☐ Dark
☐ Magic
☐ Naughty
☐ Secret

10. Which TV show featured Walter and Skyler White?

☐ Breaking Bad
☐ Dexter
☐ Orange is the New Black
☐ Game of Thrones

ANSWERS

7 Yellow. 8 BBC. 9 Magic. 10 Breaking Bad.

1 Thous shalt not commit adultery. 2 Cycling. 3. Cribbage. 4 66. 5 Black. 6 Holes.

117

QUIZ 56: GEOGRAPHY

1. On which continent is the Amazon river?
- ☐ Africa
- ☐ Europe
- ☐ North America
- ☐ South America

2. What is the chief official language of Israel?
- ☐ Arabic
- ☐ English
- ☐ American
- ☐ Hebrew

3. In which Ocean is Greenland?
- ☐ Arctic
- ☐ Atlantic
- ☐ Southern
- ☐ Pacific

4. What is the continent around the South Pole called?
- ☐ Arctic
- ☐ Antarctic
- ☐ Australasia
- ☐ Southland

5. What is the Matterhorn?
- ☐ Glacier
- ☐ Lake
- ☐ Mountain
- ☐ Sea

6. In which country is Buenos Aires?

☐ Argentina
☐ Brazil
☐ Paraguay
☐ Uruguay

7. Which country does the island of Rhodes belong to?

☐ Cyprus
☐ Greece
☐ Turkey
☐ Italy

8. Normandy is part of which country?

☐ Belgium
☐ Canada
☐ France
☐ Great Britain

9. In which World are underdeveloped countries said to be?

☐ Other
☐ Poor
☐ Second
☐ Third

10. What did Iran used to be called?

☐ Atlantis
☐ Persia
☐ Sparta
☐ Tehran

QUIZ 57

1. Which game might you be watching if you were at the Belfry?
- ☐ Bowls
- ☐ Curling
- ☐ Football
- ☐ Golf

2. Variola is more commonly called what?
- ☐ Measles
- ☐ Mumps
- ☐ Smallpox
- ☐ Whooping Cough

3. What is Diana Prince's other identity?
- ☐ Batwoman
- ☐ Catwoman
- ☐ Wonder Girl
- ☐ Wonder Woman

4. Which Scottish group took their name from a Scritti Politti lyric?
- ☐ Travis
- ☐ Ultravox
- ☐ The Waterboys
- ☐ Wet Wet Wet

5. Which musical instrument does Nigel Kennedy play?
- ☐ Cello
- ☐ Drums
- ☐ Flute
- ☐ Violin

6. After what is London's Fleet Street named?

- [ ] A battle
- [ ] Fast runners
- [ ] Fast writers
- [ ] The River Fleet

7. What is a 200th anniversary called?

- [ ] Bicentenary
- [ ] Centenary
- [ ] Double-century
- [ ] Double-ton

8. How many players are there in a basketball team?

- [ ] 4
- [ ] 5
- [ ] 6
- [ ] 7

9. On the London Underground, on which line is Knightsbridge station?

- [ ] Circle
- [ ] District
- [ ] Piccadilly
- [ ] Victoria

10. In which year did *Dr Who* first appear on BBC?

- [ ] 1959
- [ ] 1961
- [ ] 1963
- [ ] 1965

ANSWERS

1 Golf 2 Smallpox. 3 Wonder Woman. 4 Wet Wet Wet. 5 Violin. 6 The River Fleet. 7 Bicentenary. 8 5. 9 Piccadilly. 10 1963.

121

Quiz 58: History

1. Which ruler was stabbed to death in Rome in March 44 BC?
- [ ] Brutus
- [ ] Caesar
- [ ] Coriolanus
- [ ] Nero

2. Who was Henry VIII's first wife?
- [ ] Anne Boleyn
- [ ] Anne of Cleeves
- [ ] Catherine of Aragon
- [ ] Katherine Parr

3. What was the name of the first King of England and Scotland?
- [ ] Charles
- [ ] George
- [ ] James
- [ ] Henry

4. Who were massacred by the Campbells at Glencoe?
- [ ] MacDonalds
- [ ] MacDougals
- [ ] MacDufs
- [ ] MacGregors

5. Who was the famous captain of the ship the *Golden Hind*?
- [ ] Francis Chichester
- [ ] Francis Drake
- [ ] John Hawkins
- [ ] Walter Raleigh

6. From 1714 to 1830 all British monarchs were called what?

- [ ] Charles
- [ ] George
- [ ] James
- [ ] Henry

7. Which King Henry ordered the murder of Thomas Becket?

- [ ] Henry II
- [ ] Henry IV
- [ ] Henry VI
- [ ] Henry VIII

8. Who led the British forces at the Battle of Waterloo?

- [ ] Napoleon Bonaparte
- [ ] Lord Nelson
- [ ] Duke of Wellington
- [ ] Duke of York

9. Which US President was assassinated at the theatre?

- [ ] Garfield
- [ ] Lincoln
- [ ] McKinley
- [ ] Kennedy

10. Who was British monarch throughout the Second World War?

- [ ] George V
- [ ] George VI
- [ ] Edward VI
- [ ] Edward VI

ANSWERS

1 Caesar VI. 2 Catherine of Aragon. 3 James. 4 MacDonalds. 5 Francis Drake. 6 George. 7 Henry II. 8 Duke of Wellington. 9 Lincoln. 10 George VI

123

QUIZ 59

1. Who wrote the novel *The Murder of Roger Ackroyd*?
☐ Agatha Christie
☐ P. D. James
☐ Ruth Rendell
☐ Dorothy L. Sayers

2. Whom is the US state of Virginia named after?
☐ Queen Victoria
☐ Queen Elizabeth I
☐ Virginia McKenna
☐ Virginia Woolf

3. Which Elvis song has the words "you ain't never caught a rabbit"?
☐ Blue Suede Shoes
☐ Hound Dog
☐ In the Ghetto
☐ Jailhouse Rock

4. Which stimulant is found in tea and coffee?
☐ Amphetamine
☐ Caffeine
☐ Tannine
☐ Taurine

5. Which French phrase used in English means already seen?
☐ Deja vu
☐ Frou frou
☐ Parlez vous
☐ Voulez vous

6. The airline Labrador Airways is from which country?

☐ Canada
☐ Germany
☐ Poland
☐ Switzerland

7. In Cockney rhyming slang what are mince pies?

☐ Bonsai
☐ Eyes
☐ Glasses
☐ Highs

8. What type of creature is a stingray?

☐ Dog
☐ Fish
☐ Insect
☐ Snake

9. Which day of the week is Shrove once a year?

☐ Sunday
☐ Tuesday
☐ Wednesday
☐ Friday

10. In which TV series did the character René Artois appear?

☐ 'Allo 'Allo
☐ Blackadder
☐ Dad's Army
☐ Only Fools And Horses

ANSWERS

1 Agatha Christie. 2 Queen Elizabeth I. 3 Hound Dog. 4 Caffeine. 5 Deja vu.
6 Canada. 7 Eyes. 8 Fish. 9 Tuesday. 10 Allo Allo.

125

QUIZ 60

1. Who went with Christopher Robin to Buckingham Palace?

☐ Alice
☐ Alice's boyfriend
☐ Poo bear
☐ The bears

2. In which country is the city of Amritsar?

☐ Bhutan
☐ India
☐ Nepal
☐ Pakistan

3. Who wrote the novel *Rebecca*?

☐ Agathan Christie
☐ Noel Coward
☐ Daphne du Maurier
☐ Joan Fontaine

4. Moving clockwise on a dartboard what number is next to 1?

☐ 5
☐ 6
☐ 12
☐ 18

5. How many yards in a chain?

☐ 20
☐ 22
☐ 25
☐ 50

6. Who is king at the start of *A Game of Thrones*?
- [ ] Robert Baratheon
- [ ] Joffrey Baratheon
- [ ] Stannis Baratheon
- [ ] Renly Baratheon

7. Frigophobia is the fear of what?
- [ ] Being cold
- [ ] Fridges
- [ ] Ice
- [ ] Sex

8. In which game would you find a night watchman?
- [ ] Badminton
- [ ] Cricket
- [ ] Three-day eventing
- [ ] Steeplechase

9. St Winifred's School Choir sang about which relative?
- [ ] Grandad
- [ ] Grandma
- [ ] Mammy
- [ ] Dad

10. Who wrote the novel *The Water Babies*?
- [ ] Charles Kingsley
- [ ] Henry Kingsley
- [ ] Mary Kingsley
- [ ] Jesse Wilcox Smith

ANSWERS

1 Alice. 2 India. 3 Daphne du Maurier. 4 18. 5 22. 6 Robert Baratheon.
7 Being cold. 8 Cricket. 9 Grandma. 10 Charles Kingsley

127

QUIZ 61

1. What colour is a female blackbird?
- [ ] Black
- [ ] Brown
- [ ] White
- [ ] Yellow

2. In which country is the city of Antwerp?
- [ ] Belguim
- [ ] Holland
- [ ] France
- [ ] Germany

3. How many degrees in a semicircle?
- [ ] 90
- [ ] 180
- [ ] 270
- [ ] 360

4. What is a scout rally called?
- [ ] Corroboree
- [ ] Gathering
- [ ] Jamboree
- [ ] Party

5. What, according to proverb, breeds contempt?
- [ ] Deceit
- [ ] Familiarity
- [ ] Family
- [ ] Rudeness

6. What is the square root of 9?

☐ 1

☐ 3

☐ 9

☐ 29

7. What was the name of Dick Turpin's horse?

☐ Black Beauty

☐ Black Bess

☐ Black Caviar

☐ Brown Beauty

8. How is Allen Konigsberg better known?

☐ Woody Allen

☐ Bob Dylan

☐ Woody Guthrie

☐ Woody Harrelson

9. In "Cinderella", what was the pumpkin turned in to?

☐ Coach

☐ Fairy

☐ Glass slipper

☐ Horse

10. How does 7.20 p.m. appear on a 24-hour clock?

☐ 17.20

☐ 19.20

☐ 07.20

☐ 24/7

ANSWERS

1 Brown. 2 Belgium. 3 180. 4 Jamboree. 5 Familiarity. 6 3. 7 Black Bess. 8 Woody Allen. 9 Coach. 10 19.20.

129

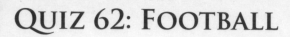

Quiz 62: Football

1. Who succeeded Alex Ferguson as Manchester United manager?
- ☐ David Beckham
- ☐ Ryan Giggs
- ☐ David Moyes
- ☐ Louis van Gaal

2. What is the colour of the strip of the Welsh national team?
- ☐ Blue
- ☐ Red
- ☐ White
- ☐ Yellow

3. Boca Juniors come from which country?
- ☐ Argentina
- ☐ Brazil
- ☐ Portugal
- ☐ Uruguay

4. Franco Baresi played 450 plus games for which Italian club?
- ☐ AC Milan
- ☐ Chievo
- ☐ Inter
- ☐ Juventus

5. Jan Ceulemans played for which country?
- ☐ Belgium
- ☐ France
- ☐ Germany
- ☐ Holland

6. Who followed Cruyff as coach at Barcelona?

☐ Glenn Hoddle
☐ Bobby Robson
☐ Louis van Haal
☐ Terry Venables

7. The Stadium of Light is home of which Portuguese club?

☐ Benfica
☐ Braga
☐ Estoril
☐ Porto

8. In which country did Pele wind down his playing career?

☐ Brazil
☐ England
☐ Spain
☐ USA

9. Gazza has NOT played club football in which of the following?

☐ England
☐ Italy
☐ Scotland
☐ Wales

10. Which country hosted the 1966 World Cup?

☐ England
☐ Germany
☐ Mexico
☐ Spain

ANSWERS

6 Robson. 7 Benfica. 8 USA. 9 Wales. 10 England.
1 David Moyes. 2 Red. 3 Argentina. 4 AC Milan. 5 Belgium.

131

QUIZ 63

1. In which country is the city of Crakow (or Kraków)?
- [ ] Germany
- [ ] Poland
- [ ] Romania
- [ ] Russia

2. In which month is St David's Day?
- [ ] January
- [ ] February
- [ ] March
- [ ] April

3. What colour is the wax covering Edam cheese?
- [ ] Black
- [ ] Red
- [ ] White
- [ ] Yellow

4. Which UK car manufacturer produced the Imp?
- [ ] Ford
- [ ] Hillman
- [ ] Humber
- [ ] Morris

5. How many ounces in a pound?
- [ ] 10
- [ ] 12
- [ ] 14
- [ ] 16

6. What is a Pontefract cake made of?
- ☐ Cheese
- ☐ Dried fruit
- ☐ Liquorice
- ☐ Oats

7. Which Donald set a world water speed record in the Lake District?
- ☐ Campbell
- ☐ Glover
- ☐ Russell
- ☐ Trump

8. Colonel Nasser nationalized which canal?
- ☐ Hoi An
- ☐ Panama
- ☐ Suez
- ☐ Venice

9. *Lord of the Flies* was written by which author William?
- ☐ Burgess
- ☐ Fowles
- ☐ Golding
- ☐ Goldman

10. Which film classification was introduced to show films were unsuitablefor the under 16s?
- ☐ A
- ☐ AA
- ☐ R
- ☐ X

ANSWERS

1 Poland. 2 March. 3 Red. 4 Hillman. 5 16. 6 Liquorice. 7 Campbell. 8 Suez. 9 Golding. 10 X.

133

1. Fidel Castro seized power in which country?

☐ Cuba
☐ Honduras
☐ Mexico
☐ Panama

2. What, according to Marilyn Monroe, were a girl's best friend?

☐ Chocolate
☐ Diamonds
☐ Dogs
☐ Men

3. Packham's Triumph and Conference are types of what?

☐ Apples
☐ Cars
☐ Pears
☐ Potatoes

4. On which hill did Fats Domino find his thrill?

☐ Blueberry
☐ Blubbery
☐ Bunker
☐ Calvary

5. In which country is the city of Durban?

☐ Australia
☐ India
☐ Pakistan
☐ South Africa

6. Which British film won nine Oscars in 1997?

☐ The English Patient
☐ Howard's End
☐ The King's Speech
☐ Silence of the Lambs

7. What is the square root of 16?

☐ 2
☐ 4
☐ 8
☐ 32

8. In which activity do you purl and cast off?

☐ Diving
☐ Fishing
☐ Knitting
☐ Power-boat racing

9. In which city were the 2000 Olympics held?

☐ Barcelona
☐ Beijing
☐ Seoul
☐ Sydney

10. Which Brit pop band were formed in Colchester?

☐ Blur
☐ Oasis
☐ Pulp
☐ Suede

ANSWERS

1 Cuba. 2 Diamonds. 3 Pears. 4 Blueberry. 5 South Africa. 6 The English Patient.
7 4. 8 Knitting. 9 Sydney. 10 Blur.

135

QUIZ 65

1. In which decade did the writer Laurie Lee die?
- ☐ 1970s
- ☐ 1980s
- ☐ 1990s
- ☐ 2000s

2. Who were the first team to win the FA Premiership?
- ☐ Blackburn Rovers
- ☐ Chelsea
- ☐ Leeds United
- ☐ Manchester United

3. In which TV programme did Florence and Zebedee appear?
- ☐ Jackanory
- ☐ The Magic Roundabout
- ☐ The Magic Garden
- ☐ Mary, Mungo and Midge

4. What do Macintosh computers use as a logo?
- ☐ Apple
- ☐ Acorn
- ☐ Banana
- ☐ Cherry

5. Miss Havisham appears in which Charles Dickens novel?
- ☐ A Tale of Two Cities
- ☐ Bleak House
- ☐ Great Expectations
- ☐ Oliver Twist

6. What colour is quartz citrine?

☐ Green
☐ Red
☐ Yellow
☐ White

7. In the 1990s, which team were Super Bowl runners-up four years in a row?

☐ Buffalo Bills
☐ Green Bay Packers
☐ Miami Dolphins
☐ San Francisco 49ers

8. Theo Walcott joined Arsenal from which club?

☐ Cardiff
☐ Chelsea
☐ Exeter
☐ Southampton

9. In which country is the city of Fez?

☐ Algeria
☐ Libya
☐ Morocco
☐ Tunisia

10. Who wrote the novel *Kidnapped*?

☐ Charles Dickens
☐ Arthur Conan Doyle
☐ Edgar Allen Poe
☐ Robert Louis Stephenson

ANSWERS

1 1990s. 2 Manchester United. 3 The Magic Roundabout. 4 Apple. 5 Great Expectations. 6 Yellow. 7 Buffalo Bills. 8 Southampton. 9 Morocco. 10 Robert Louis Stephenson.

137

QUIZ 66: ANIMAL

1. A papillon is a breed of what?
- [ ] Bird
- [ ] Butterfly
- [ ] Dog
- [ ] Moth

2. What is the term for a group of beavers?
- [ ] Chapter
- [ ] Colony
- [ ] Group
- [ ] Munch

3. Dromedary and Bactrian are types of what?
- [ ] Cat
- [ ] Camel
- [ ] Dog
- [ ] Horse

4. Which is the odd one out?
- [ ] Dodo
- [ ] Great Auk
- [ ] Colombian Grebe
- [ ] African Penguin

5. What is a male fox called?
- [ ] Canidae
- [ ] Dog
- [ ] Kid
- [ ] Vixen

6. How many teats does a cow usually have?

☐ 3
☐ 4
☐ 5
☐ 6

7. In Britain, which is the only venomous snake?

☐ Adder
☐ Asp
☐ Boa constrictor
☐ Viper

8. A jenny is a female what?

☐ Cow
☐ Donkey
☐ Elephant
☐ Horse

9. Which animal lives in an earth or sett?

☐ Badger
☐ Beaver
☐ Fox
☐ Rabbit

10. Which creature provides a mole's main source of food?

☐ Badger
☐ Earthworm
☐ Mouse
☐ Rat

ANSWERS

1 Dog. 2 Colony. 3 Camel. 4 African Penguin (the others are extinct). 5 Dog. 6 4.
7 Adder. 8 Donkey. 9 Badger. 10 Earthworm.

QUIZ 67

1. Which team did Michael Owen leave to go and play soccer in Spain?
- [ ] Ajax
- [ ] Everton
- [ ] Liverpool
- [ ] Manchester United

2. Who wrote the novel *War and Peace*?
- [ ] Anton Checkov
- [ ] Fyodor Dostoyevsky
- [ ] Leo Tolstoy
- [ ] Ivan Turgenev

3. In which country is the city of Kuala Lumpur?
- [ ] Indonesia
- [ ] Malaysia
- [ ] Phillipines
- [ ] Singapore

4. Dave Bedford is associated with which sport?
- [ ] Athletics
- [ ] Boxing
- [ ] Football
- [ ] Rowing

5. Where on the body could a cataract form?
- [ ] Arm
- [ ] Ear
- [ ] Eye
- [ ] Leg

6. What is the square root of 25?

☐ 3
☐ 5
☐ 15
☐ 25

7. Which planet is named after the Roman god of war?

☐ Mars
☐ Neptune
☐ Pluto
☐ Venus

8. On a Monopoly board, what colour is Bond Street?

☐ Blue
☐ Green
☐ Orange
☐ Yellow

9. Kurt Cobain was in which grunge group?

☐ Alice In Chains
☐ Foo Fighters
☐ Nirvana
☐ Pearl Jam

10. What does the A stand for in CIA?

☐ Agency
☐ Amalgamated
☐ Association
☐ Authority

QUIZ 68

1. Which Nobel Prize did Nelson Mandela win?
☐ Economics
☐ Literature
☐ Peace
☐ Science

2. In which month is Hallowe'en?
☐ September
☐ October
☐ November
☐ December

3. What kind of bomb contains hydrogen sulphide?
☐ Atomic bomb
☐ H bomb
☐ Stink bomb
☐ Water bomb

4. Which descriptive word is linked with the singer John Baldry?
☐ Big
☐ Long
☐ Short
☐ Tall

5. Where does an arboreal creature live?
☐ In a tree
☐ In a desert
☐ Under ground
☐ Under water

6. How many seconds in one hour?
- ☐ 360
- ☐ 1,400
- ☐ 3,600
- ☐ 7,200

7. Which Doctor had a dog called K9?
- ☐ Crippen
- ☐ Finlay
- ☐ Watson
- ☐ Who

8. Which vitamin deficiency was responsible for scurvy?
- ☐ A
- ☐ B
- ☐ C
- ☐ D

9. Which Beatle played guitar left-handed?
- ☐ John
- ☐ George
- ☐ Paul
- ☐ Ringo

10. In song, what do you pack up in your old kit bag?
- ☐ Bullets
- ☐ Ciggies
- ☐ Grub
- ☐ Troubles

ANSWERS

1 Peace. 2 October. 3 Stink bomb. 4 Long. 5 In a tree. 6 3,600. 7 Who. 8 C. 9 Paul.
10 Troubles.

143

QUIZ 69

1. In which sport is the Giro D'Italia – the Tour of Italy?
- ☐ Cycling
- ☐ Football
- ☐ Handball
- ☐ Rugby

2. Agoraphobia is the fear of what?
- ☐ Confined spaces
- ☐ Everything
- ☐ Open spaces
- ☐ Spiders

3. In which UK city did the ill-fated Millennium Dome open?
- ☐ Birmingham
- ☐ Bristol
- ☐ Glasgow
- ☐ London

4. What is the boundary of a circle called?
- ☐ Circumference
- ☐ Diameter
- ☐ Intersection
- ☐ Segment

5. In which country is the city of Stuttgart?
- ☐ Austria
- ☐ Germany
- ☐ Hungary
- ☐ Ukraine

6. Who sang with Stills, Nash and Young?

☐ Browne
☐ Crosby
☐ Dylan
☐ Morrison

7. Which Alice declared: School's Out?

☐ Cooper
☐ Guy-Blaché
☐ In Wonderland
☐ Walker

8. How many reds are there at the start of a snooker game?

☐ 10
☐ 12
☐ 13
☐ 15

9. What is the term for written or recorded defamation?

☐ Defamation of character
☐ Lies
☐ Libel
☐ Slander

10. H is the chemical symbol for which element?

☐ Hafnium
☐ Helium
☐ Holmium
☐ Hydrogen

QUIZ 70: POP ALBUMS

1. What goes after "What's the Story" in the title of Oasis's album?

☐ If you look back in anger
☐ Jackanory
☐ Mate
☐ Morning Glory

2. Who recorded *No Jacket Required*?

☐ Phil Collins
☐ Peter Gabriel
☐ Genesis
☐ Mike and the Mechanics

3. Who recorded *Dark Side of the Moon*?

☐ The Doors
☐ ELO
☐ Led Zeppelin
☐ Pink Floyd

4. Which group had a *Night at the Opera* and a *Day at the Races*?

☐ Aerosmith
☐ Marx Brothers
☐ Queen
☐ Status Quo

5. Paul McCartney was in which group for "Band on the Run"?

☐ Beatles
☐ Quarrymen
☐ Traveling Wilburys
☐ Wings

6. Mike Oldfield presented what type of Bells?

☐ Big
☐ Church
☐ Hell's
☐ Tubular

7. Who recorded *Off the Wall*?

☐ Michael Douglas
☐ Pink Floyd
☐ Janice Jackson
☐ Michael Jackson

8. Which Abba album had a French title?

☐ Deja vu
☐ N'est-ce pas
☐ Voulez vous
☐ Waterloo

9. What was the Kaiser Chiefs' debut album called?

☐ Employment
☐ Hard Work
☐ Takin' It Easy
☐ Unemployment

10. Who recorded *Rubber Soul*?

☐ Beatles
☐ Kinks
☐ Rolling Stones
☐ Bay City Rollers

ANSWERS

1 Morning Glory 2 Phil Collins. 3 Pink Floyd. 4 Queen. 5 Wings. 6 Tubular. 7 Michael Jackson. 8 Voulez vous. 9 Employment. 10 Beatles

147

QUIZ 71

1. Who had a sidekick called Tonto?

☐ Batman
☐ d'Artagnon
☐ The Lone Ranger
☐ Dick Turpin

2. In which country is the city of São Paulo?

☐ Argentina
☐ Brazil
☐ Mexico
☐ Panama

3. Who sang with Dolly Parton on "Islands in the Stream"?

☐ Jim Reeves
☐ Kenny Rogers
☐ Don Williams
☐ Boxcar Willie

4. What name is given to a yacht with two hulls?

☐ Catamaran
☐ Monohull
☐ Trimaran
☐ Skiff

5. In song, which road is taken to get to Scotland "afore ye"?

☐ Bottom
☐ High
☐ Low
☐ Top

6. In theatre, what is traditionally the main colour in a Pierrot costume?

☐ Black

☐ Pink

☐ Red

☐ White

7. How is actor Ronald Moodnick better known?

☐ Dustin Hoffman

☐ Ron Moody

☐ Al Pacino

☐ Oliver Reed

8. Who in the 50s had "Rock Island Line" as his first million-seller?

☐ Lonnie Donegan

☐ Billy Fury

☐ Tommy Steele

☐ Frankie Vaughn

9. What is 75 per cent of 200?

☐ 75

☐ 100

☐ 150

☐ 175

10. Who is Scotland's patron saint?

☐ Andrew

☐ Bruce

☐ Cuithbairt

☐ Donald

ANSWERS

1 The Lone Ranger. 2 Brazil. 3 Kenny Rogers. 4 Catamaran. 5 Low. 6 White. 7 Ron Moody. 8 Lonnie Donegan. 9 150. 10 Andrew.

149

QUIZ 72

1. In which Disney film does "The Bare Necessities" appear?

☐ Cinderella
☐ Fantasia
☐ The Jungle Book
☐ The Rescuers

2. Manuel and Sybil appeared in which TV series?

☐ Bless this House
☐ Fawlty Towers
☐ Monty Python's Flying Circus
☐ On the Buses

3. Love apple is an old-fashioned name for what?

☐ Apple
☐ Cider
☐ Sweet
☐ Tomato

4. Veteran rockers Rossi and Parfitt are in which group?

☐ ACDC
☐ Queen
☐ Rolling Stones
☐ Status Quo

5. In which country is the city of Zürich?

☐ Austria
☐ Germany
☐ Poland
☐ Switzerland

6. "It's Not Unusual" was the first No. 1 for which singer?
- ☐ Elton John
- ☐ Tom Jones
- ☐ Cliff Richard
- ☐ Tommy Steele

7. Which chess piece can change direction in a normal move?
- ☐ Bishop
- ☐ King
- ☐ Knight
- ☐ Queen

8. Meteorophobia is the fear of what?
- ☐ Meteors
- ☐ Metronomes
- ☐ Scarecrows
- ☐ Weather

9. Which country did the Righteous Brothers come from?
- ☐ Australia
- ☐ South Africa
- ☐ UK
- ☐ USA

10. In song, what did my true love send me on the second day of Christmas?
- ☐ Drummers drumming
- ☐ French hens
- ☐ Partridge in a pear tree
- ☐ Turtle doves

ANSWERS

1 The Jungle Book. 2 Fawlty Towers. 3 Tomato. 4 Status Quo. 5 Switzerland. 6 Tom Jones. 7 Knight. 8 Meteors. 9 USA. 10 Turtle doves.

151

QUIZ 73

1. Which UK car manufacturer produced the Zodiac?

☐ Ford
☐ Hillman
☐ Humber
☐ Rolls-Royce

2. What is Formosa now called?

☐ Malaysia
☐ Singapore
☐ Taipei
☐ Taiwan

3. In *The Simpsons* who or what is Duff?

☐ Beer
☐ The mayor
☐ Mo's bar
☐ The policeman

4. What is a third of 1,200?

☐ 300
☐ 350
☐ 400
☐ 600

5. Who formed a trio with Paul and Mary?

☐ James
☐ John
☐ Maria
☐ Peter

6. With which event in athletics was Geoff Capes associated?
- ☐ Hammer
- ☐ Javelin
- ☐ Shot put
- ☐ Truck pulling

7. In the US, who presented *The Tonight Show* for 30 years?
- ☐ Johnny Carson
- ☐ Jimmy Fallon
- ☐ Jay Leno
- ☐ David Letterman

8. Which Bob invented the Moog Synthesiser?
- ☐ Droog
- ☐ Moog
- ☐ Waters
- ☐ Wilson

9. How many metres in four kilometres?
- ☐ 400
- ☐ 4,000
- ☐ 40,000
- ☐ 400,000

10. Which George starred in *Minder*?
- ☐ Cole
- ☐ Daley
- ☐ Jones
- ☐ Waterman

ANSWERS

1 Ford. 2 Taiwan. 3 Beer. 4 400. 5 Peter. 6 Shot put. 7 Johnny Carson. 8 Moog. 9 4,000. 10 Cole.

153

Quiz 74: Sports

1. The green jacket is presented to the winner of which event?
☐ Crufts
☐ Grand National
☐ US Open
☐ Wimbledon

2. In boxing, what weight division is directly below heavyweight?
☐ Cruiserweight
☐ Lightweight
☐ Middleweight
☐ Welterweight

3. In horse racing, in which month is the Melbourne Cup held?
☐ September
☐ October
☐ November
☐ December

4. Kim Clijsters and Justine Henin-Hardenne are from which country?
☐ Belgium
☐ France
☐ Holland
☐ Germany

5. The 2004 Summer Olympics took place in which country?
☐ Australia
☐ China
☐ Greece
☐ England

6. Which player signed for Real Madrid from Tottenham Hotspur in 2013?

☐ Emmanuel Adebayor
☐ Gareth Bale
☐ Rafael van der Vaart
☐ Aaron Ramsey

7. How often is cycling's Tour of Spain held?

☐ Annually
☐ Every two years
☐ Every five years
☐ Monthly

8. A cricket umpire extends both arms horizontally to signal what?

☐ 4
☐ 6
☐ Out
☐ Wide

9. In golf, what is the term for two under par for a hole?

☐ Albatross
☐ Birdie
☐ Eagle
☐ Tunder

10. What sport do the Pittsburgh Steelers play?

☐ American Football
☐ Baseball
☐ Basketball
☐ Ice Hockey

ANSWERS

1 US Open. 2 Cruiserweight. 3 November. 4 Belgium. 5 Greece. 6 Gareth Bale.
7 Annually. 8 Wide. 9 Eagle. 10 American Football.

155

QUIZ 75

1. Which rock legend died at his mansion Graceland?
- ☐ Jimi Hendrix
- ☐ Freddie Mercury
- ☐ Jim Morrison
- ☐ Elvis Presley

2. Haile Selassie was deposed in which country?
- ☐ Egypt
- ☐ Ethiopia
- ☐ Jamaica
- ☐ Sudan

3. The tennis superstar Bjorn Borg came from which country?
- ☐ Denmark
- ☐ Holland
- ☐ Norway
- ☐ Sweden

4. What type of a rectangle has four equal sides and angles?
- ☐ Conical
- ☐ Isocoles
- ☐ Regular
- ☐ Square

5. The airline Iberia is from which country?
- ☐ Italy
- ☐ Portugal
- ☐ Scotland
- ☐ Spain

6. Which general made a last stand at Little Big Horn?

☐ Custer
☐ Eisenhower
☐ Napoleon
☐ Patton

7. The characters Fletcher and Godber appeared in which TV series?

☐ Bird
☐ Birds of a Feather
☐ Porridge
☐ Straight Up

8. Who was singer with Roxy Music?

☐ David Bowie
☐ Brian Ferry
☐ Robert Palmer
☐ David Sylvian

9. What is the square root of 64?

☐ 4
☐ 8
☐ 16
☐ 32

10. Timbuktu is on the edge of which desert?

☐ Ghobi
☐ Kalahari
☐ Namib
☐ Sahara

QUIZ 76

1. What is sauerkraut?
- [ ] German beer
- [ ] Pickled cabbage
- [ ] Pickled cucumber
- [ ] Sausage

2. The characters Rigsby and Miss Jones appeared in which TV series?
- [ ] Bless This House
- [ ] The Rise and Fall of Reginald Perrin
- [ ] Rising Damp
- [ ] Robin's Nest

3. Jeremy Bates is associated with which sport?
- [ ] Badminton
- [ ] Squash
- [ ] Table tennis
- [ ] Tennis

4. What's the fruity link with the name of William III of England?
- [ ] Apple
- [ ] Banana
- [ ] Lemon
- [ ] Orange

5. In history, which harbour in the US had a famous Tea Party?
- [ ] Boston
- [ ] Miami
- [ ] New York
- [ ] San Francisco

6. In which country is the city of Auckland?

☐ Australia
☐ New Zealand
☐ South Africa
☐ USA

7. On a Monopoly board, what colour is Piccadilly?

☐ Dark blue
☐ Light blue
☐ Green
☐ Yellow

8. On a London Underground map, what colour is the Piccadilly line?

☐ Dark blue
☐ Light blue
☐ Green
☐ Yellow

9. Glenn Hoddle finished his playing career with which club?

☐ Barcelona
☐ Chelsea
☐ Monaco
☐ Tottenham Hotspur

10. Sydney Carton appears in which Charles Dickens novel?

☐ A Tale of Two Cities
☐ Bleak House
☐ Oliver Twist
☐ Nicholas Nickleby

1 Pickled cabbage. 2 Rising Damp. 3 Tennis. 4 Orange. 5 Boston. 6 New Zealand. 7 Yellow. 8 Dark blue. 9 Chelsea. . 10 A Tale of Two Cities.

159

QUIZ 77

1. In which month is St Patrick's Day?
☐ February
☐ March
☐ April
☐ May

2. What is a quarter of 180?
☐ 45
☐ 90
☐ 100
☐ 135

3. Dr Hook sang about whose mother?
☐ Mine
☐ Sandra's
☐ Sylvia's
☐ Your

4. What was the name of the piano-playing Muppet dog?
☐ Big Bird
☐ Ralph
☐ Rolph
☐ Rowlf

5. Who was awarded a supper of brown bread and butter?
☐ Beau Peep
☐ Little Miss Muffet
☐ Little Tommy Tucker
☐ Mary

6. Which Elton John song includes the words "Goodbye Norma Jean"?

☐ Candle In The Wind
☐ Nikita
☐ I'm Still Standing
☐ Your Song

7. Which movie Mrs Robinson died in 2005?

☐ Anne Bancroft
☐ Elaine Robinson
☐ Iris Robinson
☐ Katharine Ross

8. Who had the award-winning 1999 album *Surrender*?

☐ Chemical Brothers
☐ Dust Brothers
☐ Fatboy Slim
☐ The Prodigy

9. Which John wrote the play *Look Back In Anger*?

☐ Amis
☐ Osborne
☐ Pinter
☐ Sillitoe

10. Which Ronnie starred in *Open All Hours*?

☐ Barker
☐ Biggs
☐ Corbett
☐ Scott

ANSWERS

1 March. 2 45. 3 Sylvia's. 4 Rowlf. 5 Little Tommy Tucker. 6 Candle In The Wind. 7 Anne Bancroft. 8 Chemical Brothers. 9 Osborne. 10 Barker.

161

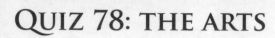

QUIZ 78: THE ARTS

1. Diaghilev was associated with which branch of the arts?
☐ Ballet
☐ Film-making
☐ Music
☐ Painting

2. Guiseppe Verdi is most famous for which type of musical work?
☐ Opera
☐ Orchestral symphonies
☐ Pop song
☐ String quartet

3. Who wrote *HMS Pinafore*?
☐ Gilbert & Sullivan
☐ Rodgers & Hammerstein
☐ Sondheim
☐ Verdi

4. What was the nationality of the pianist and composer Claude Debussy?
☐ American
☐ Belgian
☐ French
☐ German

5. Which musical instrument did Stéphane Grappelli play?
☐ Cello
☐ Drums
☐ Guitar
☐ Violin

6. If you receive a Tony you have been performing in which country?
- [ ] England
- [ ] France
- [ ] Italy
- [ ] USA

7. What kind of entertainment did Barnum call "the Greatest Show on Earth"?
- [ ] Circus
- [ ] Electric guitar
- [ ] Football
- [ ] Opera

8. How many sisters were in the title of the play by Chekhov?
- [ ] 2
- [ ] 3
- [ ] 4
- [ ] 5

9. A balalaika originates from which country?
- [ ] Cyprus
- [ ] Egypt
- [ ] Greece
- [ ] Turkey

10. In which city is the Bolshoi Theatre?
- [ ] Gdansk
- [ ] Kiev
- [ ] Moscow
- [ ] New York

ANSWERS

1 Ballet. 2 Opera. 3 Gilbert & Sullivan. 4 French. 5 Violin. 6 USA. 7 Circus. 8 3. 9 Greece. 10 Moscow.

163

QUIZ 79

1. In which country is the city of Baghdad?

☐ Iran
☐ Iraq
☐ Kuwait
☐ Syria

2. O is the chemical symbol for which element?

☐ Cobalt
☐ Osmium
☐ Oxygen
☐ Palladium

3. Who won an Oscar for Best Actor in *My Fair Lady*?

☐ Richard Burton
☐ Jamie Harris
☐ Noel Harrison
☐ Rex Harrison

4. From which fruit is the drink kirsch made?

☐ Apple
☐ Cherry
☐ Lemon
☐ Lime

5. In ten-pin bowling, how many pins are there in the back row?

☐ 3
☐ 4
☐ 5
☐ 6

6. Who is Colin Dexter's most famous creation?

☐ Cracker
☐ Dixon of Dock Green
☐ Inspector Morse
☐ Miss Marple

7. Who is R2D2's robot companion in *Star Wars*?

☐ C3PO
☐ Chewbacca
☐ Princess Leia
☐ Luke Skywalker

8. In which country was the 2014 football World Cup held?

☐ Brazil
☐ Germany
☐ Mexico
☐ USA

9. How is the rock guitarist William Perks better known?

☐ Keith Richards
☐ Mick Taylor
☐ Ronnie Wood
☐ Bill Wyman

10. Arachnophobia is the fear of what?

☐ Airplane
☐ Insects
☐ Spiders
☐ Whales

ANSWERS

1 Iraq. 2 Oxygen. 3 Rex Harrison. 4 Cherry. 5 4. 6 Inspector Morse. 7 C3PO.
8 Brazil. 9 Bill Wyman. 10 Spiders.

165

QUIZ 80

1. The character Nick Cotton appeared in which TV soap?
☐ A Country Practice
☐ Home & Away
☐ Neighbours
☐ The Sullivans

2. Who was the Premier League's top scorer in the 2013–14 season?
☐ Luis Suarez
☐ Daniel Sturridge
☐ Sergio Agüero
☐ Olivier Giroud

3. How many league goals did (question 2, above) score?
☐ 27
☐ 29
☐ 31
☐ 33

4. How many grams in a kilogram?
☐ 12
☐ 100
☐ 1,000
☐ 10,000

5. Queen Anne Boleyn was said to possess an extra what on her body?
☐ Ear
☐ Eye
☐ Finger
☐ Toe

6. What is 5 cubed?
- ☐ 5
- ☐ 25
- ☐ 125
- ☐ 1,025

7. Which number follows S Club in the band's title?
- ☐ 1
- ☐ 5
- ☐ 7
- ☐ 50

8. In the 90s, who had a No. 1 with "Vogue"?
- ☐ Cher
- ☐ Debbie Harry
- ☐ Madonna
- ☐ Beyoncé

9. What does the Q stand for in IQ?
- ☐ Quota
- ☐ Quotient
- ☐ Quiz
- ☐ Quintessential

10. Indira Gandhi International airport is in which country?
- ☐ Afghanistan
- ☐ India
- ☐ Pakistan
- ☐ Sri Lanka

ANSWERS

1 Neighbours. 2 Luis Suárez. 3 31. 4 1,000. 5 Finger. 6 125. 7 7. 8 Madonna. 9 Quotient. 10 India.

167

QUIZ 81

1. What colour are Holland's international soccer shirts?

☐ Black
☐ Green
☐ Orange
☐ White

2. Which team did Wigan beat in the 2013 FA Cup Final?

☐ Arsenal
☐ Manchester City
☐ Manchester United
☐ Sheffield Wednesday

3. The character Captain Kirk appeared in which TV series?

☐ Battlestar Galactica
☐ Soldier Soldier
☐ Star Trek
☐ Star Wars

4. Which toy was Hornby most famous for?

☐ Racing cars
☐ Spinning tops
☐ Train sets
☐ Video games

5. What is the name of Tom Cruise's character in the *Mission Impossible* films?

☐ Jack Harmon
☐ Ethan Hunt
☐ Jim Phelps
☐ Jack Reacher

6. Which Gloria recorded "I Will Survive"?

☐ Cake
☐ Estefan
☐ Gaynor
☐ Hunniford

7. The airline Olympic is from which country?

☐ Canada
☐ Greece
☐ Turkey
☐ USA

8. Which pets featured on the programmes with Barbara Woodhouse?

☐ Cats
☐ Dogs
☐ Mice
☐ Snakes

9. Which UK car manufacturer produced the Dolomite?

☐ Ford
☐ Humber
☐ Morris
☐ Triumph

10. In which country is the city of Bilbao?

☐ Greece
☐ Honduras
☐ Mexico
☐ Spain

— ANSWERS

1 Orange. 2 Manchester City. 3 Star Trek. 4 Train sets. 5 Ethan Hunt. 6 Gaynor. 7 Greece. 8 Dogs. 9 Triumph. 10 Spain

QUIZ 82: HOBBIES AND

1. In which game would you have a pitcher's mound and an outfield?

☐ American Football
☐ Baseball
☐ Netball
☐ Rounders

2. Which card game is also called vingt-et-un?

☐ Blackjack
☐ Go Johnny Go Go Go Go
☐ Poker
☐ Pontoon

3. Where are the Crown Jewels housed?

☐ Bank of England
☐ Buckingham Palace
☐ Tower of London
☐ Westminster Abbey

4. What colour flag is awarded by the EC to beaches of a certain standard?

☐ Black
☐ Blue
☐ Red
☐ Yellow

5. What would you collect if you collected Clarice Cliff?

☐ Insects
☐ Matchboxes
☐ Pottery
☐ Stamps

LEISURE

6. What is the junior version of Lego called?

- ☐ Baby-lego
- ☐ Brio
- ☐ Kreo
- ☐ Smallo

7. Which is the odd one out?

- ☐ Doodlebug
- ☐ Tango
- ☐ Tap
- ☐ Waltz

8. What would your hobby be if you bought a first-day cover?

- ☐ Birds
- ☐ Insects
- ☐ Tents
- ☐ Stamps

9. Europe's first Disney theme park was built near which city?

- ☐ Berlin
- ☐ Gdansk
- ☐ Paris
- ☐ Stockholm

10. What type of museum has Imperial in front of its name in London?

- ☐ Imperial Bird Museum
- ☐ Imperial Design Museum
- ☐ Imperial Transport Museum
- ☐ Imperial War Museum

ANSWERS

1 Baseball. 2 Pontoon. 3 Tower of London. 4 Blue. 5 Pottery. 6 Brio. 7 Doodlebug (the others are dances). 8 Stamps. 9 Paris. 10 War.

171

QUIZ 83

1. Which London underground station was named after a football club?
- [ ] Arsenal
- [ ] Buckhurst Hill
- [ ] Camden Town
- [ ] West Ham

2. On which day are hot cross buns traditionally eaten?
- [ ] Boxing Day
- [ ] Easter Sunday
- [ ] Good Friday
- [ ] Shrove Tuesday

3. Who wrote the novel *Lucky Jim*?
- [ ] Kingsley Amis
- [ ] Martin Amis
- [ ] Philip Larkin
- [ ] Hayley Mills

4. On a Monopoly board, what colour is Old Kent Road?
- [ ] Light blue
- [ ] Brown
- [ ] Green
- [ ] White

5. What is Kampuchea now called?
- [ ] Cambodia
- [ ] Malaysia
- [ ] Singapore
- [ ] Thailand

6. How many degrees in a right angle?

- [ ] 15
- [ ] 45
- [ ] 90
- [ ] 180

7. Which group had a No. 1 with "Hey Jude"?

- [ ] The Beatles
- [ ] Jimi Hendrix Experience
- [ ] The Kinks
- [ ] The Rolling Stones

8. Who wrote the novel *Jane Eyre*?

- [ ] Anne Brontë
- [ ] Branwell Brontë
- [ ] Charlotte Brontë
- [ ] Emily Brontë

9. What is 3 cubed?

- [ ] 1
- [ ] 9
- [ ] 27
- [ ] 333

10. How many sides does a trapezium have?

- [ ] 4
- [ ] 5
- [ ] 6
- [ ] 7

ANSWERS

1 Arsenal. 2 Good Friday. 3 Kingsley Amis. 4 Brown. 5 Cambodia. 6 90. 7 The Beatles. 8 Charlotte Brontë. 9 27. 10 4.

173

QUIZ 84

1. How is Marie McDonald McLaughlin Lawrie better known?
- [ ] Cilla Black
- [ ] Lulu
- [ ] Helen Shapiro
- [ ] Sandie Shaw

2. What destroyed millions of British trees in October 1987?
- [ ] Disease
- [ ] Fire
- [ ] Flood
- [ ] Hurricane

3. What do you ride on if you take part in three-day eventing?
- [ ] Bicycle
- [ ] Cattle
- [ ] Horse
- [ ] Motorbike

4. What colour gloves does a snooker referee wear?
- [ ] Black
- [ ] Red
- [ ] White
- [ ] Yellow

5. Which word means faster than the speed of sound?
- [ ] Atomic
- [ ] Subsonic
- [ ] Supersonic
- [ ] Superspeedy

6. The first Harry Potter novel concerned the Philospher's what?

☐ Glasses
☐ Goblet
☐ Stone
☐ Wand

7. Which colourless, odourless light gas is used to lift airships?

☐ Chlorine
☐ Helium
☐ Hydrogen
☐ Methane

8. What is the oldest university in the USA?

☐ Brown
☐ Harvard
☐ Stanford
☐ Yale

9.What is the main colour of Nigeria's football strip?

☐ Blue
☐ Green
☐ Red
☐ White

10. Sid Vicious was a member of which punk band?

☐ Buzzcocks
☐ The Damned
☐ Stiff Little Fingers
☐ Sex Pistols

QUIZ 85

1. In which country is the city of Calgary?
- [ ] Canada
- [ ] Israel
- [ ] Syria
- [ ] USA

2. Who wrote the play *Pygmalion*?
- [ ] Euripedes
- [ ] George Bernard Shaw
- [ ] Sophocles
- [ ] Oscar Wilde

3. How would 71 be shown in Roman numerals?
- [ ] CXXI
- [ ] LXXI
- [ ] XXXCI
- [ ] VIVI

4. Jack Regan and George Carter appeared in which TV series?
- [ ] Minder
- [ ] New Tricks
- [ ] The Sweeney
- [ ] Thieftakers

5. In which month is St George's Day?
- [ ] March
- [ ] April
- [ ] May
- [ ] June

6. Which bird gave Fleetwood Mac their first No. 1?

- ☐ Albatross
- ☐ Big
- ☐ Free
- ☐ Penguin

7. What type of book links Bridget Jones and Samuel Pepys?

- ☐ Bible
- ☐ Black
- ☐ Diary
- ☐ Log

8. What instrument did Fats Waller play?

- ☐ Drums
- ☐ Piano
- ☐ Saxophone
- ☐ Trumpet

9. In mammals, the Asian elephant is second but man has the longest – what?

- ☐ Hair
- ☐ Legs
- ☐ Lifespan
- ☐ Trunk

10. The characters Alf, Else and Rita appeared in which TV series?

- ☐ Golden Girls
- ☐ On the Buses
- ☐ Steptoe and Son
- ☐ Till Death Do Us Part

ANSWERS

1 Canada. 2 George Bernard Shaw. 3 LXXI. 4 The Sweeney. 5 April. 6 Albatross. 7 Diary. 8 Piano. 9 Lifespan. 10 Till Death Do Us Part

QUIZ 86: ANIMALS

1. What is a chameleon capable of changing?
- ☐ Colour
- ☐ Shape
- ☐ Skin
- ☐ Smell

2. What is the aquatic larva of an amphibian more commonly called?
- ☐ Froglet
- ☐ Nymph
- ☐ Tadpole
- ☐ Toad

3. What does a reptile shed in the process of sloughing?
- ☐ Legs
- ☐ Skin
- ☐ Tail
- ☐ Teeth

4. What is another name for snake poison?
- ☐ Antidote
- ☐ Juice
- ☐ Snoison
- ☐ Venom

5. The aardvark is a native of which continent?
- ☐ Asia
- ☐ Africa
- ☐ Europe
- ☐ North America

6. Which is the only mammal able to fly?
- ☐ Bat
- ☐ Emu
- ☐ Moth
- ☐ Ostrich

7. Which type of dark-coloured bear is the largest?
- ☐ Black
- ☐ Brown
- ☐ Giant
- ☐ Grizzly

8. What is the main diet of hedgehogs?
- ☐ Fish
- ☐ Insects
- ☐ Mice
- ☐ Worms

9. What is the fastest land animal?
- ☐ Cheetah
- ☐ Leopard
- ☐ Lion
- ☐ Man

10. What colour is a chow chow's tongue?
- ☐ Black
- ☐ Blue
- ☐ Pink
- ☐ Red

ANSWERS

1 Colour. 2 Tadpole 4. 3 Skin. 4 Venom. 5 Africa. 6 Bat. 7 Grizzly. 8 Insects. 9 Cheetah. 10 Blue.

QUIZ 87

1. Who wrote the novel *Gridlock*?
- ☐ Rowan Atkinson
- ☐ Richard Curtis
- ☐ Ben Elton
- ☐ Ian Lafrenais

2. Which team won the 2014 FA Cup?
- ☐ Arsenal
- ☐ Hull
- ☐ Manchester City
- ☐ Wigan

3. How to you write one thousand in Roman numerals?
- ☐ M
- ☐ MX
- ☐ MXM
- ☐ MXC

4. What name is given to a two-coloured oblong cake covered with almond paste?
- ☐ Battenberg
- ☐ Black Forest
- ☐ Dundee
- ☐ Simnel

5. In which country is the city of Dresden?
- ☐ Austria
- ☐ Germany
- ☐ Hungary
- ☐ Poland

6. Who wanted to ask the Wizard of Oz for courage?

☐ Cowardly Lion
☐ Scarecrow
☐ Tin Man
☐ Dorothy

7. In past times, what would a gentleman keep in his fob pocket?

☐ Knife
☐ Wallet
☐ Watch
☐ Whistle

8. What kind of creature is a cabbage white?

☐ Bird
☐ Butterfly
☐ Leopard
☐ Worm

9. Which US emergency phone number is also the name of a band to make No. 1?

☐ 24/7
☐ 808
☐ 911
☐ E17

10. How many gills in a pint?

☐ 4
☐ 8
☐ 10
☐ 12

ANSWERS

1 Ben Elton. 2 Arsenal. 3 M. 4 Battenberg. 5 Germany. 6 Cowardly Lion. 7 Watch. 8 Butterfly. 9 911. 10 4.

181

QUIZ 88

1. What is stored in a tantalus?
- ☐ Decanters
- ☐ Napkins
- ☐ Salt and pepper shakers
- ☐ Tants

2. Claustrophobia is the fear of what?
- ☐ Enclosed spaces
- ☐ Open spaces
- ☐ Spiders
- ☐ Santa claus

3. Who wrote the novel *Black Beauty*?
- ☐ Frances Hodgson Burnett
- ☐ Lucy Kemp-Welch
- ☐ Anna Sewell
- ☐ Brian Sewell

4. In France, what is the abbreviation for Monsieur?
- ☐ M.
- ☐ Me.
- ☐ Mr.
- ☐ Msr.

5. What is the square root of 121?
- ☐ 11
- ☐ 12
- ☐ 12.1
- ☐ 121

6. Which John starred in *Bergerac*?

☐ Nettles
☐ Hawkins
☐ Hughes
☐ Shaw

7. Who won an Oscar for Best Actress in *The Silence of the Lambs*?

☐ Jodie Foster
☐ Helen Hunt
☐ Ashley Judd
☐ Julianne Moore

8. What is the traditional accompaniment to haggis on Burns Night?

☐ Cream
☐ Mashed banana
☐ Mashed sweed (neeps)
☐ Whisky

9. A4 is a size of what?

☐ Glass
☐ Paper
☐ Shoes
☐ Trousers

10. What name is given to a starter dish of sliced raw vegetables?

☐ Crudities
☐ Prawn cocktail
☐ Sashimi
☐ Salad

1 Decanters. 2 Enclosed spaces. 3 Anna Sewell. 4 M. 5 11. 6 Nettles. 7 Jodie Foster. 8 Mashed sweed. 9 Paper. 10 Crudities.

183

QUIZ 89

1. Eric Clapton, Ginger Baker and Jack Bruce formed which group?
- [ ] Cream
- [ ] Herman's Hermits
- [ ] Rolling Stones
- [ ] The Yardbirds

2. How many square feet in a square yard?
- [ ] 6
- [ ] 9
- [ ] 12
- [ ] 15

3. Who wrote the novel "Dead Cert"?
- [ ] Dan Brown
- [ ] Dick Francis
- [ ] Frederick Forsyth
- [ ] Stieg Larsson

4. In the 80s, who had a No. 1 with "Karma Chameleon"?
- [ ] Boy George
- [ ] Culture Club
- [ ] Kajagoogoo
- [ ] Colour By Numbers

5. Galileo Galilei airport is in which country?
- [ ] France
- [ ] Italy
- [ ] Portugal
- [ ] Spain

6. Who was the long-time leader of the Mothers of Invention?

☐ Captain Beefheart
☐ Don Van Vliet
☐ Dweezil Zappa
☐ Frank Zappa

7. Which John won an Oscar for Best Actor in *True Grit*?

☐ Galt
☐ Steed
☐ Stewart
☐ Wayne

8. What are farfalle, pansotti and rigati?

☐ Italian cities
☐ Pasta shapes
☐ Pasta sauces
☐ Types of rice

9. What is the dog called in a Punch and Judy show?

☐ Bonzo
☐ Bully
☐ Basher
☐ Toby

10. *Holby City* is a spin-off from which medical drama?

☐ Angels
☐ Casualty
☐ ER
☐ Grey's Anatomy

ANSWERS

1 Cream. 2 9. 3 Dick Francis. 4 Culture Club. 5 Italy. 6 Frank Zappa.
7 Wayne. 8 Pasta shapes. 9 Toby. 10 Casualty

Quiz 90: Soul Music

1. The Four Tops had only one British No 1. What was it?

☐ I Can't Help Myself (Sugar Pie, Honey Bunch)
☐ It's The Same Old Song
☐ Reach Out I'll Be There
☐ Standing In The Shadows Of Love

2. Who was the boss of Tamla Motown?

☐ Marvin Gaye
☐ Berry Gordy
☐ Smokey Robinson
☐ Diana Ross

3. Who was sitting on the dock of the bay?

☐ Solomon Burke
☐ Al Green
☐ Wilson Pickett
☐ Otis Redding

4. Who, according to Jimmy Ruffin, "had love that has now departed"?

☐ The Brokenhearted
☐ The Lonely
☐ The sad and lonely
☐ The shadows

5. Who is known as "The Godfather of Soul"?

☐ James Brown
☐ Ray Charles
☐ Berry Gordy
☐ Michael Jackson

6. Which group backed Martha Reeves?

☐ The Supremes
☐ Three Degrees
☐ The Pips
☐ The Vandellas

7. Lionel Ritchie was in which soul band?

☐ Alabama
☐ Commodores
☐ Good Charlotte
☐ Natural High

8. Which soul singer married Whitney Houston in 1992?

☐ Ricky Bell
☐ Bobby Brown
☐ Johnny Gill
☐ Ralph Tresvant

9. What was Smokey Robinson's real first name?

☐ David
☐ Paul
☐ Peter
☐ William

10. Which hour did Cropper and Pickett write about?

☐ Daybreak
☐ Longest
☐ Midnight
☐ Shortest

ANSWERS

1 Reach Out I'll Be There. 2 Berry Gordy. 3 Otis Redding. 4 The Brokenhearted. 5 James Brown. 6 The Vandellas. 7 Commodores. 8 Bobby Brown. 9 William. 10 Midnight.

187

QUIZ 91

1. Who wrote the book *The Hitch Hiker's Guide to the Galaxy*?
- ☐ Douglas Adams
- ☐ Isaac Asimov
- ☐ Neil Gaiman
- ☐ Terry Pratchett

2. What is a sheep-shank?
- ☐ An animal
- ☐ A knot
- ☐ A place in Australia
- ☐ A wine

3. Who played Pussy Galore in *Goldfinger*?
- ☐ Honor Blackman
- ☐ Shirley Eaton
- ☐ Diana Rigg
- ☐ Linda Thorson

4. How many portraits are carved into Mount Rushmore?
- ☐ 3
- ☐ 4
- ☐ 5
- ☐ 6

5. Which Ministry is the MoD?
- ☐ Defence
- ☐ Delight
- ☐ Digging
- ☐ Division

6. Zr is the chemical symbol for which element?
- ☐ Gold
- ☐ Silver
- ☐ Zinc
- ☐ Zirconium

7. Which country did the late comedian Dave Allen come from?
- ☐ England
- ☐ Ireland
- ☐ Scotland
- ☐ Wales

8. In which month is All Saints' Day?
- ☐ October
- ☐ November
- ☐ December
- ☐ January

9. How many square inches in a square foot?
- ☐ 3
- ☐ 12
- ☐ 144
- ☐ 1,024

10. Who was queen of the Roman Gods?
- ☐ Hera
- ☐ Juno
- ☐ Mars
- ☐ Uni

————— ANSWERS

7 Ireland. 8 November. 9 144. 10 Juno

1 Douglas Adams. 2 Knot. 3 Honor Blackman. 4 4. 5 Defence. 6 Zirconium.

189

QUIZ 92

1. Adnams brewery is located in which county?
- ☐ Avon
- ☐ Essex
- ☐ London
- ☐ Suffolk

2. In which country is South America's highest mountain?
- ☐ Argentina
- ☐ Brazil
- ☐ Chile
- ☐ Ecuador

3. In which country is the city of Istanbul?
- ☐ Greece
- ☐ Italy
- ☐ Sweden
- ☐ Turkey

4. Which standard begins, "They asked me how I knew, my true love was true"?
- ☐ I Only Have Eyes For You
- ☐ I Wanna Know What Love Is
- ☐ My One And Only Love
- ☐ Smoke Gets In Your Eyes

5. Eddie Merckx was a record breaker in which sport?
- ☐ Cycling
- ☐ Rowing
- ☐ Running
- ☐ Waterskiing

6. What colour is Noddy's hat?
- [ ] Black
- [ ] Blue
- [ ] Grey
- [ ] Red

7. Who wrote the novel *Tess of the D'Urbervilles*?
- [ ] Charles Dickens
- [ ] George Eliot
- [ ] Thomas Hardy
- [ ] Louisa May Alcott

8. In the 70s, who had a No. 1 with "Long-Haired Lover from Liverpool"?
- [ ] Alan Osmond
- [ ] Donny Osmond
- [ ] Jimmy Osmond
- [ ] Marie Osmond

9. Which Bruce starred in *Moonlighting*?
- [ ] Lee
- [ ] Springsteen
- [ ] Stallone
- [ ] Willis

10. Henry Cecil is associated with which sport?
- [ ] Boxing
- [ ] Formula 1
- [ ] Horse racing
- [ ] Rugby

ANSWERS

1. Suffolk, 2 Argentina, 3 Turkey, 4 Smoke Gets In Your Eyes, 5 Cycling, 6 Blue, 7 Thomas Hardy, 8 Jimmy Osmond, 9 Willis, 10 Horse racing.

191

QUIZ 93

1. Which piece of furniture is Benjamin Franklin credited with creating?
☐ Cot
☐ Eames chair
☐ Rocking chair
☐ Reclining chair

2. What is a group of five performers called?
☐ Trio
☐ Quartet
☐ Quintet
☐ Sextet

3. Who is Cockney Chas's singing partner?
☐ Chuck
☐ Dave
☐ Jim
☐ Ozzy

4. Which is the largest country in Great Britain?
☐ England
☐ Ireland
☐ Scotland
☐ Wales

5. Who wrote *Pilgrim's Progress*?
☐ John Bunyan
☐ Geoffry Chaucer
☐ John Milton
☐ John Owen

6. Which is the only bird capable of flying all day without flapping its wings?

☐ Albatross
☐ Blackhawk
☐ Eagle
☐ Vulture

7. Which 60s group was formed by the Wilson brothers?

☐ The Beach Boys
☐ The Byrds
☐ Jan & Dean
☐ The Kinks

8. In which country is the Jasper National Park?

☐ Canada
☐ France
☐ UK
☐ USA

9. What do you dislike if you are misocapnic?

☐ Bread
☐ Fruit
☐ Open spaces
☐ Tobacco smoke

10. In which country did judo develop?

☐ China
☐ India
☐ Japan
☐ South Korea

ANSWERS

1 Rocking chair. 2 Quintet. 3 Dve. 4 England. 5 John Bunyan. 6 Albatross. 7 The Beach Boys. 8 Canada. 9 Tobacco smoke. 10 Japan.

193

QUIZ 94: WAR MOVIES

1. Which Hollywood legend played Kurtz in *Apocalypse Now*?
☐ Marlon Brando
☐ James Dean
☐ Robert Duvall
☐ Orson Welles

2. For which Robert de Niro film was "Cavatina" the theme music?
☐ The Deer Hunter
☐ Full Metal Jacket
☐ Platoon
☐ Taxi Driver

3. Who won an Oscar as the Colonel in *The Bridge on the River Kwai*?
☐ Kirk Douglas
☐ Alec Guinness
☐ David Lean
☐ Laurence Olivier

4. In *The Colditz Story* what type of building was Colditz?
☐ Bungalow
☐ Campsite
☐ Castle
☐ Tower

5. What type of soldiers were the four Britons in *The Wild Geese*?
☐ Commandos
☐ Deserters
☐ Mercenaries
☐ Snipers

6. Whose café was a meeting place for war refugees in *Casablanca*?

- ☐ Louis's
- ☐ Rick's
- ☐ Sam's
- ☐ Victor's

7. Who wrote the novel on which *Where Eagles Dare* was based?

- ☐ Desmond Bagley
- ☐ Jack Higgins
- ☐ Alistair MacLean
- ☐ Robert Ludlum

8. In *A Town Like Alice* what does "Alice" refer to?

- ☐ A cat
- ☐ Alice Holt
- ☐ Alice Springs
- ☐ Alice in Wonderland

9. Who directed *Born on the Fourth of July*?

- ☐ Tom Cruise
- ☐ Brian De Palma
- ☐ Willem Dafoe
- ☐ Oliver Stone

10. In which country is *The Killing Fields* set?

- ☐ Cambodia
- ☐ China
- ☐ Korea
- ☐ Vietnam

ANSWERS

1 Marlon Brando. 2 The Deer Hunter. 3 Alec Guinness. 4 Castle. 5 Mercenaries. 6 Rick's. 7 Alistair MacLean. 8 Alice Springs. 9 Oliver Stone. 10 Cambodia.

195

QUIZ 95

1. In the initials FIFA, what does the first F stand for?
- ☐ Fairplay
- ☐ Fanatics
- ☐ Federation
- ☐ Football

2. Who wrote the controversial novel *The Satanic Verses*?
- ☐ Isabel Allende
- ☐ J.M. Coetzee
- ☐ Padma Lakshmi
- ☐ Salman Rushdie

3. Which country's stamps have featured the word Helvetia?
- ☐ Holland
- ☐ Hungary
- ☐ Scotland
- ☐ Switzerland

4. A nepotist favours what type of people?
- ☐ Men
- ☐ Tall people
- ☐ Their relatives
- ☐ Women

5. Billingsgate Market was famous for what sort of food?
- ☐ Fish
- ☐ Flowers
- ☐ Fruit
- ☐ Vegetables

6. Who or what was Genevieve in the classic film of the same name?

- ☐ A car
- ☐ A dead person
- ☐ A fairy
- ☐ A train

7. A lift for food in a restaurant is known as what kind of waiter?

- ☐ Clever
- ☐ Dumb
- ☐ Heavy
- ☐ Silent

8. The humerus is in what part of the body?

- ☐ Back
- ☐ Head
- ☐ Lower leg
- ☐ Upper arm

9. Which country did Galileo come from?

- ☐ Italy
- ☐ Portugal
- ☐ Spain
- ☐ West Germany

10. In which month is Christmas in Australia?

- ☐ October
- ☐ November
- ☐ December
- ☐ January

ANSWERS

1 Federation. 2 Salman Rushdie. 3 Switzerland. 4 Their relatives. 5 Fish. 6 A car. 7 Dumb. 8 Upper arm. 9 italy. 10 December.

197

QUIZ 96

1. Which board game has a Genus Edition?
☐ Monopoly
☐ Cluedo
☐ Kensington
☐ Trivial Pursuit

2. What do you hit with a racket in badminton?
☐ Ball
☐ Puck
☐ Shuttlecock
☐ Spring

3. What was the traditional colour for Aran wool?
☐ Black
☐ Blue
☐ Cream
☐ Green

4. What sort of toy was a Cabbage Patch?
☐ Board game
☐ Car
☐ Doll
☐ Fancy dress

5. How many balls are used in a game of billiards?
☐ 3
☐ 5
☐ 9
☐ 15

6. How many members make up a water polo team?
- ☐ 5
- ☐ 6
- ☐ 7
- ☐ 8

7. In Scrabble what colour are the double-word-score squares?
- ☐ Green
- ☐ Pink
- ☐ Red
- ☐ Yellow

8. Which is the odd one out?
- ☐ Foil
- ☐ Epée
- ☐ Sabre
- ☐ Club

9. Which game is called the national pastime in the USA?
- ☐ Baseball
- ☐ Basketball
- ☐ (American) Football
- ☐ Ice Hockey

10. If you were watching someone on a PGA tour what would you be watching?
- ☐ Golf
- ☐ Football
- ☐ Table tennis
- ☐ Tennis

ANSWERS

1 Trivial Pursuit. 2 Shuttlecock. 3 Cream. 4 Doll. 5 3. 6 7.
7 Pink. 8 Club – the others are all fencing sword names. 9 Baseball. 10 Golf.

199

QUIZ 97

1. Who wrote the novel *A Town Like Alice*?
- [ ] Iain Banks
- [ ] Charles Dickens
- [ ] John Irving
- [ ] Nevil Shute

2. In which sport was the Twenty20 Cup introduced?
- [ ] Cricket
- [ ] Football
- [ ] Rugby
- [ ] Tennis

3. What are the words in the shortest verse of the Bible?
- [ ] Amen
- [ ] And there was light
- [ ] Jesus wept
- [ ] Titter ye not

4. Which Tom was the first player to be twice Footballer of the Year?
- [ ] Finney
- [ ] Lofthouse
- [ ] Matthews
- [ ] Wright

5. In which country is the city of Tijuana?
- [ ] Belize
- [ ] Cuba
- [ ] Honduras
- [ ] Mexico

6. Which ancient calculator used a frame and beads?

☐ Abacus
☐ Adder
☐ Counter
☐ Tallymark

7. How many players are there in a field hockey team?

☐ 9
☐ 10
☐ 11
☐ 12

8. If March 1 is a Saturday, what day is April 1?

☐ Saturday
☐ Sunday
☐ Monday
☐ Tuesday

9. Cotton denotes which wedding anniversary?

☐ 1st
☐ 2nd
☐ 3rd
☐ 5th

10. In which month is Independence Day in the USA?

☐ April
☐ May
☐ July
☐ August

ANSWERS

8 Tuesday. 9 1st. 10 July.

1 Nevil Shute. 2 Cricket. 3 Jesus wept. 4 Finney. 5 Mexico. 6 Abacus. 7 11.

201

QUIZ 98: MEDIA

1. Name Mary Quant's shop, which revolutionized fashion in the 1960s?

☐ Bazaar
☐ Bizarre
☐ Mary's
☐ Sex

2. Which mountain was first climbed by Edward Whymper in 1865?

☐ Eiger
☐ Everest
☐ Matterhorn
☐ Mt Rainier

3. In fiction, Michael Henchard became mayor of which town?

☐ Casterbridge
☐ Castle Rock
☐ Middlemarch
☐ Sandbourne

4. In music, what is meant by pianissimo?

☐ On a piano
☐ Slowly
☐ Very loud
☐ Very soft

5. What popular drink was known in China as early as 2737 BC?

☐ Beer
☐ Coffee
☐ Coca-cola
☐ Tea

6. On how many stone tablets were the Ten Commandments engraved?

☐ 1
☐ 2
☐ 3
☐ 4

7. Riyadh is the capital of which country?

☐ Dubai
☐ Iceland
☐ Oman
☐ Saudi Arabia

8. Which insect sometimes eats its male mate during copulation?

☐ Ant
☐ Ladybird
☐ Praying Mantis
☐ Spider

9. Which famous gardener helped landscape Blenheim and Stowe?

☐ Capability Brown
☐ Beth Chatto
☐ Edith Wharton
☐ Andrew Jackson Downing

10. In which city would you find the Blue Mosque?

☐ Ankara
☐ Baghdad
☐ Cairo
☐ Istanbul

ANSWERS

1 Bazaar. 2 Matterhorn. 3 Casterbridge. 4 Very soft. 5 Tea. 6 2. 7 Saudi Arabia. 8 Praying Mantis. 9 Capability Brown. 10 Istanbul.

203

QUIZ 99

1. Which present-day country do we associate with the Magyars?
☐ Holland
☐ Hungary
☐ Madagascar
☐ Malaysia

2. Chris Patten was the last British Governor of where?
☐ Cairo
☐ China
☐ Gibraltar
☐ Hong Kong

3. In which month is St Swithin's Day?
☐ April
☐ May
☐ June
☐ July

4. In Cockney rhyming slang, what are "plates of meat"?
☐ Feet
☐ Plates
☐ Seats
☐ Sweets

5. The Kalahari desert is in which continent?
☐ Africa
☐ Asia
☐ Europe
☐ South America

6. The character Michelle Fowler appeared in which TV soap?

☐ Brookside
☐ Coronation Street
☐ Crossroads
☐ EastEnders

7. Who wrote the novel *The Hobbit*?

☐ C.S. Lewis
☐ George R.R. Martin
☐ J.R.R. Tolkien
☐ J.K. Rowling

8. Who made up the trio with Emerson and Lake?

☐ Blake
☐ Nash
☐ Palmer
☐ Young

9. What number is cubed to give the answer 8?

☐ 2
☐ 4
☐ 6
☐ 8

10. Which UK car manufacturer produced the Midget?

☐ Ford
☐ Hillman
☐ MG
☐ Triumph

ANSWERS

1 Hungary. 2 Hong Kong. 3 July. 4 Feet. 5 Africa. 6 EastEnders. 7 JRR Tolkien. 8 Palmer. 9 2. 10 MG.

205

QUIZ 100

1. With what type of entertainment is Marcel Marceau associated?
☐ Ballet
☐ Mime
☐ Movies
☐ Theatre

2. Thierry Henry joined Arsenal from which club?
☐ AC Milan
☐ Ajax
☐ Barcelona
☐ Juventus

3. In which British city is the station Temple Meads?
☐ Bath
☐ Birmingham
☐ Bristol
☐ Manchester

4. If you have "mal de mer" what are you suffering from?
☐ Vertigo
☐ Sea-sickness
☐ Car-sickness
☐ Morning sickness

5. What kind of farm did George Orwell write about?
☐ Animal
☐ Communist
☐ Funny
☐ Nut

6. In proverb, there is "many a slip 'twixt cup" and what?

☐ Bottle
☐ Decanter
☐ Glass
☐ Lip

7. Who composed the piece of music known as the "Moonlight Sonata"?

☐ Bach
☐ Beethoven
☐ Chopin
☐ Mozart

8. What name is given in law to a person who makes a will?

☐ Executor
☐ Probate
☐ Testator
☐ Willer

9. What colour were the shirts of Mussolini's Italian Fascists?

☐ Black
☐ Blue
☐ Red
☐ White

10. Which animal appears on the front of a British passport with a lion?

☐ Donkey
☐ Griffin
☐ Sheep
☐ Unicorn

ANSWERS

1 Mime. 2 Juventus. 3 Bristol. 4 Sea-sickness. 5 Animal. 6 Lip. 7 Beethoven. 8 Testator. 9 Black. 10 Unicorn

QUIZ 101

1. Who was elected Governor of California in 2003?
- [ ] Clint Eastwood
- [ ] Sylvester Stallone
- [ ] Arnold Schwarzenegger
- [ ] Harry Tasker

2. Which of the seven deadly sins begins with G?
- [ ] Glamour
- [ ] Gluttony
- [ ] Greed
- [ ] Pride

3. What was Ghana's former name?
- [ ] Congo
- [ ] Ghanaia
- [ ] Gold Coast
- [ ] Liberia

4. The Dutch royal family acquired its name from which French town?
- [ ] Lyon
- [ ] Orange
- [ ] Orleans
- [ ] Paris

5. Which of the following is the corncrake?
- [ ] Bird
- [ ] Mammal
- [ ] Reptile
- [ ] Insect

6. Which tanker suffered a severe oil spill in Alaska in 1989?

☐ Amoco Cadiz
☐ Burmah Agate
☐ Exxon Valdez
☐ Khark 5

7. Where is the pituitary gland?

☐ Brain
☐ Buttock
☐ Genitals
☐ Mouth

8. In which country are the Angel Falls?

☐ Kenya
☐ South Africa
☐ Tanzania
☐ Venezuela

9. Which metal is the best conductor of electricity?

☐ Brass
☐ Gold
☐ Iron
☐ Silver

10. What name is given to the thousands of small bodies that orbit the Sun?

☐ Asteroids
☐ Meteorites
☐ Satellites
☐ Sunspots

ANSWERS

1 Arnold Schwarzenegger. 2 Gluttony. 3 Gold Coast. 4 Orange. 5. Bird.
6 Exxon Valdez. 7 Brain. 8 Venezuela. 9 Silver. 10 Asteroids

209

QUIZ 102: LITERATURE

1. Who wrote *The Firm* and *The Pelican Brief*?
- [ ] James Brown
- [ ] David Baldacci
- [ ] John Grisham
- [ ] James Patterson

2. What is the first name of the novelist A. S. Byatt?
- [ ] Anita
- [ ] Annabella
- [ ] Antonia
- [ ] Arthur

3. In *Alice in Wonderland* what price did the Mad Hatter have on his hat?
- [ ] 5 guineas
- [ ] 10/6
- [ ] 10s
- [ ] 99p

4. How is adventure writer David Cornwell better known?
- [ ] John Le Carré
- [ ] Frederick Forsyth
- [ ] Graham Greene
- [ ] Robert Ludlum

5. Which town is the main setting for the Cadfael novels?
- [ ] Birmingham
- [ ] Derby
- [ ] Shrewsbury
- [ ] Telford

6. What was the job of Mellors in *Lady Chatterley's Lover*?

☐ Carpenter
☐ Gamekeeper
☐ Gardener
☐ Hunter

7. What is the name of Bernard Cornwell's hero, played on TV by Sean Bean?

☐ Aubrey
☐ Clive
☐ Eddard
☐ Sharpe

8. Who created the detective Maigret?

☐ Bruno Cremer
☐ Agatha Christie
☐ Allan Massie
☐ Georges Simenon

9. Who wrote the tales on which the film *The Jungle Book* was based?

☐ Roald Dahl
☐ Charles Dickens
☐ Rudyard Kipling
☐ Mark Twain

10. In which country was the best-seller *Wild Swans* set?

☐ China
☐ Japan
☐ Korea
☐ Mongolia

————————————————————————— ANSWERS

1 John Grisham. 2 Antonia. 3 10/6. 4 John Le Carré. 5 Shrewsbury. 6 Gamekeeper. 7 Sharpe. 8 Georges Simenon. 9 Kipling. 10 China.

211

QUIZ 103

1. Which instrument did Franz Liszt play?
- ☐ Cello
- ☐ Flute
- ☐ Piano
- ☐ Violin

2. In which year were East and West Germany unified?
- ☐ 1988
- ☐ 1989
- ☐ 1990
- ☐ 1991

3. Where was the treaty signed that established the EEC?
- ☐ Kyoto
- ☐ Lisbon
- ☐ Nice
- ☐ Rome

4. Who won the first Rugby Union World Cup, held in 1987?
- ☐ Australia
- ☐ Great Britain
- ☐ New Zealand
- ☐ South Africa

5. Who wrote the play *Waiting for Godot*?
- ☐ Samuel Beckett
- ☐ Bertold Brecht
- ☐ Eugene Ionesco
- ☐ Harold Pinter

6. What nationality was Hans Christian Andersen?
- ☐ Danish
- ☐ Estonian
- ☐ Norwegian
- ☐ Swedish

7. In which country was Rudyard Kipling born?
- ☐ England
- ☐ India
- ☐ Ireland
- ☐ Pakistan

8. Who shared a Nobel Prize for physics with his son?
- ☐ William Bragg
- ☐ Dorothy Hodgkin
- ☐ Max von Laue
- ☐ Joseph John Thomson

9. Who painted "The Night Watch?"
- ☐ da Vinci
- ☐ Rembrandt
- ☐ Rubens
- ☐ Van Gogh

10. On which circuit is motor racing's Grand Prix d'Endurance run?
- ☐ Brands Hatch
- ☐ Hungaroring
- ☐ Le Mans
- ☐ Nurburgring

ANSWERS

1 Piano. 2 1990. 3 Rome. 4 New Zealand. 5 Beckett. 6 Danish. 7 India. 8 Bragg. 9 Rembrandt. 10 Le Mans.

213

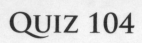

QUIZ 104

1. Who famously sailed on HMS Beagle?
☐ Charles Darwin
☐ Ferdinand Magellan
☐ Isaac Newton
☐ Marco Polo

2. What is 10 cubed?
☐ 100
☐ 1,000
☐ 10,000
☐ 100,000

3. Tom Thumb and Little Gem are types of what?
☐ Carrot
☐ Lettuce
☐ Pea
☐ Potato

4. What is Ceylon now called?
☐ Assam
☐ Bangladesh
☐ Myanmar
☐ Sri Lanka

5. Diamond denotes which wedding anniversary?
☐ 20th
☐ 50th
☐ 60th
☐ 75th

6. A merino is what kind of creature?
- ☐ Camel
- ☐ Cat
- ☐ Llama
- ☐ Sheep

7. In the 70s, who had a No. 1 with "Bright Eyes"?
- ☐ Art Garfunkel
- ☐ Paul Simon
- ☐ Peters and Lee
- ☐ Simon and Garfunkel

8. Blake and Krystle Carrington appeared in which TV series?
- ☐ Dallas
- ☐ Dancing Days
- ☐ Dynasty
- ☐ Soap

9. In tennis, what name is given to a score of 40-40?
- ☐ 40-all
- ☐ Deuce
- ☐ Love
- ☐ Tie

10. In Greek mythology, who was god of the sun?
- ☐ Apollo
- ☐ Ares
- ☐ Mars
- ☐ Zeus

ANSWERS

1 Charles Darwin. 2 1,000. 3 Lettuce. 4 Sri Lanka. 5 60th. 6 Sheep. 7 Art Garfunkel. 8 Dynasty. 9 Deuce. 10 Apollo.

215

QUIZ 105

1. What is Terry Wogan's real first name?
☐ David
☐ James
☐ Michael
☐ Patrick

2. What name was given to the 19th-century group who wrecked machines?
☐ Industrialists
☐ Luddites
☐ Smashers
☐ Wreckers

3. What is the name of Orson Welles' first film?
☐ Citizen Kane
☐ The Magnificent Ambersons
☐ War of the Worlds
☐ Wuthering Heights

4. Which river runs through the Grand Canyon?
☐ Colorado
☐ Columbia
☐ Mississippi
☐ Ohio

5. Which drug is derived from the willow, Salix alba?
☐ Aspirin
☐ Cocaine
☐ Penicillin
☐ Alka-Seltzer

6. Other than the Odyssey, which work is Homer famed for?

- [ ] The 300
- [ ] Jason and the Argonauts
- [ ] The Iliad
- [ ] The Wasps

7. Name the art of making decorative lacework with knotted threads?

- [ ] Knitting
- [ ] Knotting
- [ ] Macramé
- [ ] Weaving

8. Which indoor game was invented by British Army Officers in India in 1875?

- [ ] Billiards
- [ ] Chess
- [ ] Pool
- [ ] Snooker

9. Philip Glass wrote an opera about which scientist?

- [ ] Marie Curie
- [ ] Albert Einstein
- [ ] Stephen Hawking
- [ ] Isaac Newton

10. Which group consisted of Les, Eric, Woody, Alan and Derek?

- [ ] Bay City Rollers
- [ ] Mud
- [ ] Racey
- [ ] Showaddywaddy

ANSWERS

1 Michael. 2 Luddites. 3 Citizen Kane. 4 Colorado. 5 Aspirin. 6 Iliad. 7 Macramé. 8 Snooker. 9 Einstein. 10 Bay City Rollers.

QUIZ 106: WINE

1. Claret wine is produced in the region surrounding which French city?
☐ Beaune
☐ Bordeaux
☐ Lyon
☐ Toulouse

2. What would be the term to describe a dry champagne?
☐ Brut
☐ Demi-sec
☐ Sec
☐ Tête de cuvée

3. Which white wine grape variety is most common in California?
☐ Cabernet blanc
☐ Chardonnay
☐ Merlot blanc
☐ Muscat

4. Retsina is native to which country?
☐ Cyprus
☐ Greece
☐ Italy
☐ Turkey

5. In which country is Rioja produced?
☐ Italy
☐ Spain
☐ Portugal
☐ France

6. What is a crate of twelve bottles of wine called?

- ☐ Box
- ☐ Case
- ☐ Crate
- ☐ Pack

7. Which of the following is NOT a size of wine bottle?

- ☐ Balthazar
- ☐ Melchior
- ☐ Piccolo
- ☐ Salmanazar

8. How are fizzy wines, other than champagnes, described?

- ☐ Bubbly
- ☐ Pétillant
- ☐ Prosecco
- ☐ Sparkling

9. In which area of Italy is Chianti Classico produced?

- ☐ Abruzzo
- ☐ Lazio
- ☐ Tuscany
- ☐ Umbria

10. What type are most of the wines from France's Anjou region?

- ☐ Red
- ☐ Rosé
- ☐ Sparkling
- ☐ White

ANSWERS

1 Bordeaux. 2 Brut. 3 Chardonnay. 4 Greece. 5 Spain. 6 Case. 7 Melchior. 8 Sparkling. 9 Tuscany. 10 Rosé.

219

QUIZ 107

1. How many yards in a furlong?
- ☐ 180
- ☐ 200
- ☐ 220
- ☐ 250

2. Putin became head of state of which country?
- ☐ Poland
- ☐ Romania
- ☐ Russia
- ☐ Ukraine

3. Which country does the drink ouzo come from?
- ☐ Cyprus
- ☐ Greece
- ☐ Macedonia
- ☐ Turkey

4. How many times do you sing "jingle" in a chorus of jingle bells?
- ☐ 5
- ☐ 6
- ☐ 7
- ☐ 8

5. In which country is the city of Gothenburg?
- ☐ Denmark
- ☐ Finland
- ☐ Iceland
- ☐ Sweden

6. A mazurka is a type of what?
- [ ] Car
- [ ] Dance
- [ ] Fruit
- [ ] Train

7. On the Swedish flag what is the colour of the cross?
- [ ] Blue
- [ ] Red
- [ ] White
- [ ] Yellow

8. What type of angles are greater than 90 but less than 180 degrees?
- [ ] Acute
- [ ] Equilateral
- [ ] Obtuse
- [ ] Right

9. What colour goes before Sabbath and Box in group names?
- [ ] Black
- [ ] Blue
- [ ] Yellow
- [ ] White

10. In 2003, Jemini were the first UK act to do what in the Eurovision Song Contest?
- [ ] Come second
- [ ] Get more than 150 points
- [ ] Get no points
- [ ] Win twice

ANSWERS

1 220. 2 Russia. 3 Greece. 4 6. 5 Sweden. 6 Dance. 7 Yellow. 8 Obtuse. 9 Black. 10 Get no points.

Quiz 108

1. Who captained England in the famous 5–1 victory in Germany in 2001?
- [ ] David Beckham
- [ ] Stephen Gerrard
- [ ] Gary Lineker
- [ ] Wayne Rooney

2. Obstetrics is the study of what?
- [ ] Bones
- [ ] Brainwaves
- [ ] Childbirth
- [ ] Weight

3. In proverb speech is silver but what is golden?
- [ ] Gold
- [ ] A rumour
- [ ] Silence
- [ ] A tongue

4. Which London station would you arrive at if you travelled from Ipswich?
- [ ] Kings Cross
- [ ] Liverpool Street
- [ ] St Pancras
- [ ] Waterloo

5. What fruit are you said to be if you are accompanying a courting couple?
- [ ] Apple
- [ ] Gooseberry
- [ ] Raspberry
- [ ] Strawberry

6. Frederick the Great was king of which country?

- ☐ Germany
- ☐ Hungary
- ☐ Prussia
- ☐ Russia

7. Before going solo Beyoncé fronted which female band?

- ☐ Destiny's Child
- ☐ En Vogue
- ☐ Girls Aloud
- ☐ TLC

8. What type of creature is a painted lady?

- ☐ Bird
- ☐ Butterfly
- ☐ Fish
- ☐ Sheep

9. What does a misogynist hate?

- ☐ Authority
- ☐ Children
- ☐ Men
- ☐ Women

10. What name is given to animals that eat grass and plants?

- ☐ Herbivore
- ☐ Omnivore
- ☐ Vegan
- ☐ Vegetarian

ANSWERS

1 David Beckham. 2 Childbirth. 3 Silence. 4 Liverpool Street. 5 Gooseberry. 6 Prussia. 7 Destiny's Child. 8 Butterfly. 9 Women. 10 Herbivore.

223

QUIZ 109

1. Which cathedral has the highest spire in Britain?
- [ ] Christ Church, Oxford
- [ ] Salisbury
- [ ] Southwark
- [ ] St Paul's

2. Who sang "Hey, babe, take a walk on the wild side"?
- [ ] David Bowie
- [ ] Iggy Pop
- [ ] Lou Reed
- [ ] Andy Warhol

3. In geography, which term means the joining of two rivers?
- [ ] Confluence
- [ ] Delta
- [ ] Estuary
- [ ] Rill

4. Which musical note follows fah?
- [ ] Doh
- [ ] Lah
- [ ] Soh
- [ ] Ti

5. How many phases of the moon are there in a lunar month?
- [ ] 1
- [ ] 2
- [ ] 4
- [ ] 12

6. What on your body would a trichologist be concerned with?

☐ Bones

☐ Eyes

☐ Hair

☐ Skin

7. In the board game Cluedo what is the name of the Reverend?

☐ Black

☐ Blue

☐ Green

☐ Red

8. What have you done if you have committed patricide?

☐ Betrayed your country

☐ Murdered your brother

☐ Murdered your father

☐ Murdered your mother

9. In the Bible, where was the traveller going to in the parable of the Good Samaritan?

☐ Canaan

☐ Jaffa

☐ Jericho

☐ Jerusalem

10. What colour are Aylesbury ducks?

☐ Blue

☐ Brown

☐ White

☐ Yellow

1 Salisbury. 2 Lou Reed. 3 Confluence. 4 Soh. 5 4. 6 Hair. 7 Green. 8 Murdered your father. 9 Jericho. 10 White.

Quiz 110: Fish

1. Where is a fish's caudal fin?
- ☐ Gill cover
- ☐ Mouth
- ☐ Nostrils
- ☐ Tail

2. What sort of fish is a skipjack?
- ☐ Dolphin
- ☐ Shark
- ☐ Trout
- ☐ Tuna

3. Tinca tinca is the Latin name of which fish?
- ☐ Cod
- ☐ Dorado
- ☐ Marlin
- ☐ Tench

4. What is the world's largest fish?
- ☐ Blue whale
- ☐ Herring
- ☐ Whale shark
- ☐ Sturgeon

5. What colour is a live lobster?
- ☐ Blue/black
- ☐ Orange
- ☐ Red
- ☐ White

6. How many arms does a squid have?

- [ ] 4
- [ ] 8
- [ ] 10
- [ ] 12

7. From which part of the cod is a beneficial oil produced?

- [ ] Eye
- [ ] Liver
- [ ] Mouth
- [ ] Stomach

8. What is pisciculture?

- [ ] Fish cloning
- [ ] Fishing
- [ ] Fish rearing
- [ ] Fish paté

9. What sort of fish is a dogfish?

- [ ] Eel
- [ ] Freshwater
- [ ] Small shark
- [ ] Whale

10. Which type of crab lives in hollow objects such as snail shells?

- [ ] Littoral crabs
- [ ] Deep-sea crabs
- [ ] Land crabs
- [ ] Hermit crabs

ANSWERS

1 Tail. 2 Tuna 3 Tench. 4 Whale shark. 5 Blue/black.
6 10 limbs (8 arms, 2 tentacles). 7 Liver. 8 Fish rearing. 9 Small shark. 10 Hermit.

227

QUIZ 111

1. In Sudoku, what is the total of a square containing each number used once?

- [ ] 9
- [ ] 18
- [ ] 45
- [ ] 81

2. Which device is used on a guitar fretboard to raise the pitch of the strings?

- [ ] Capo
- [ ] Nut
- [ ] Tremolo
- [ ] Whammy bar

3. Who was the British king at the start of the First World War?

- [ ] Edward VII
- [ ] Edward VIII
- [ ] George IV
- [ ] George V

4. In imperial measurement, how many yards are in a chain?

- [ ] 4
- [ ] 10
- [ ] 11
- [ ] 22

5. With what do you play a vibraphone?

- [ ] Drumsticks
- [ ] Fingers
- [ ] Plastic sticks
- [ ] Small mallets

6. Which Spanish king abdicated in 2014?

- ☐ Charles I
- ☐ Franco
- ☐ Felipe
- ☐ Juan Carlos I

7. In literature, how many Arabian Nights were there?

- ☐ 101
- ☐ 1,000
- ☐ 1,001
- ☐ 1,000,001

8. In which war was the Battle of Jutland?

- ☐ Boer War
- ☐ Korean War
- ☐ World War I
- ☐ World War II

9. What is the square root of 169?

- ☐ 11
- ☐ 12
- ☐ 13
- ☐ 14

10. What was added to rum to make the drink grog?

- ☐ Milk
- ☐ Orange juice
- ☐ Sea water
- ☐ Water

1 45 (numbers 1 to 9). 2 Capo. 3 George V. 4 22. 5 Small mallets. 6 Juan Carlos I. 7 1,001. 8 World War I. 9 13. 10 Water

229

QUIZ 112

1. In London where is Poet's Corner?
☐ Buckingham Palace
☐ Hyde Park
☐ Regent's Park
☐ Westminster Abbey

2. Which of the following do you use dice to play?
☐ Hopscotch
☐ Poker
☐ Snakes-and-ladders
☐ Whist

3. In which month is Michaelmas Day?
☐ August
☐ September
☐ October
☐ November

4. In which English county would you find the coastal resort of California?
☐ Cornwall
☐ Devon
☐ Kent
☐ Norfolk

5. Who was the British member of the Monkees?
☐ Micky Dolenz
☐ Davy Jones
☐ Michael Nesmith
☐ Peter Tork

6. From which wood were longbows made?

☐ Birch
☐ Cedar
☐ Pine
☐ Yew

7. Of which country are Madeira and the Azores a part?

☐ Italy
☐ Portugal
☐ Russia
☐ Spain

8. In a poem by Edward Lear, what was peculiar about the "Pobble"?

☐ He ate nothing but honey
☐ He had no toes
☐ He had a beautiful pea-green boat
☐ He married an owl

9. What is or was a tin lizzie?

☐ Irish rock band
☐ Model T Ford car
☐ Queen Elizabeth I
☐ Type of bath

10. What name is given to the unit of electrical power?

☐ Amp
☐ Gigabyte
☐ Volt
☐ Watt

ANSWERS

1 Westminster Abbey. 2 Snakes-and-ladders. 3 September. 4 Norfolk. 5 Davy Jones. 6 Yew. 7 Portugal. 8 He had no toes. 9 Model T Ford. 10 Watt.

231

QUIZ 113

1. According to the proverb what do drowning men clutch?
- [ ] Buoys
- [ ] Lifebelts
- [ ] Straws
- [ ] Wood

2. What is a copper's nark?
- [ ] Car
- [ ] Sandwich
- [ ] Spy or informer
- [ ] Truncheon

3. What was the sequel to the popular children's picture book *The Gruffalo* called?
- [ ] The Gruffalittle
- [ ] The Gruffalo's Child
- [ ] Return of the Gruffalo
- [ ] Stick Man

4. In which Shakespeare play is Shylock introduced?
- [ ] As You Like It
- [ ] Coriolanus
- [ ] The Merchant of Venice
- [ ] Romeo and Juliet

5. In pop, who was King of the Wild Frontier?
- [ ] Adam Ant
- [ ] Davey Crockett
- [ ] Elvis
- [ ] Michael Jackson

6. Of which US state is Boston the capital?

- [ ] Massachusetts
- [ ] Mississippi
- [ ] New York
- [ ] Vermont

7. What did people do with Oxford bags?

- [ ] Carry things in them
- [ ] Drag them on the floor
- [ ] Drive them
- [ ] Wear them

8. In which city is Sacré Coeur?

- [ ] Brussels
- [ ] Luxembourg
- [ ] Marseille
- [ ] Paris

9. What is Sean Connery's real first name?

- [ ] Jack
- [ ] Jim
- [ ] Shaun
- [ ] Thomas

10. Which country hosted the 2014 World Cup?

- [ ] Argentina
- [ ] Brazil
- [ ] Germany
- [ ] Uruguay

1 Straws. 2 Spy or informer. 3 The Gruffalo's Child. 4 The Merchant of Venice. 5 Adam Ant. 6 Massachusetts. 7 Wear them – they were trousers. 8 Paris. 9 Thomas. 10 Brazil.

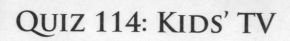

Quiz 114: Kids' TV

1. In which country is *Balamory* set?
- ☐ England
- ☐ Ireland
- ☐ Scotland
- ☐ Wales

2. Which village's postmistress is called Mrs Goggins?
- ☐ Balamory
- ☐ Biker Grove
- ☐ Greendale
- ☐ Trumpton

3. What is Rastamouse's group called?
- ☐ Bandulu
- ☐ Bagga Ts
- ☐ Da Easy Crew
- ☐ Nuff Song Posse

4. Which of the following is not from *In the Night Garden*?
- ☐ Makka Pakka
- ☐ Ragdolly Anna
- ☐ Upsy Daisy
- ☐ Wottingers

5. Which family had a daily help called Mrs Scrubbitt?
- ☐ Bill and Ben
- ☐ Crystal Tipps and Alistair
- ☐ The Flumps
- ☐ The Woodentops

6. What are the star creatures in *Paw Patrol*?

☐ Cats
☐ Dogs
☐ Lions
☐ Tigers

7. Who had magical adventures and lived at 52 Festive Road?

☐ Mr Benn
☐ Mr Happy
☐ Rod Hull and Emu
☐ Roobarb

8. In which show did the Muppets first appear?

☐ Blue Peter
☐ Fraggle Rock
☐ The Muppet Show
☐ Sesame Street

9. What was the registration number of Lady Penelope's pink Rolls in *Thunderbirds*?

☐ FAB1
☐ PINK1
☐ LADY P
☐ P1

10. Which of the following was NOT a singer on *Rainbow*?

☐ Dave
☐ Freddy
☐ Jane
☐ Rod

ANSWERS

1 Scotland. 2 Greendale. 3 Da Easy Crew. 4 Ragdolly Anna. 5 The Woodentops. 6 Dogs. 7 Mr Benn. 8 Sesame Street. 9 FAB 1. 10 Dave.

QUIZ 115

1. What nationality was detective writer Ngaio Marsh?
- [ ] British
- [ ] Australian
- [ ] South African
- [ ] New Zealander

2. Where did William III defeat a French and Irish army in 1690?
- [ ] Battle of Bantry Bay
- [ ] Battle of the Boyne
- [ ] Battle of Fleurus
- [ ] Battle of Lund

3. In the 1990s, which British manager won successive titles with PSV Eindhoven?
- [ ] Glenn Hoddle
- [ ] Roy Hodgson
- [ ] Bobby Robson
- [ ] Terry Venables

4. What was American inventor Thomas Edison's middle name?
- [ ] Alan
- [ ] Alva
- [ ] Emmanuel
- [ ] Elvis

5. What does hydrogen combine with to form water?
- [ ] Carbon
- [ ] Chlorine
- [ ] Oxygen
- [ ] Sulphur

6. Which cartoon cat is the creation of Jim Davis?

☐ The Cheshire Cat

☐ Felix

☐ Garfield

☐ Top Cat

7. What was the true vocation of the detective in the stories by G. K. Chesterton?

☐ Catholic priest

☐ Builder

☐ Butcher

☐ Doctor

8. Whom did Orpheus attempt to rescue from the underworld?

☐ Apollo

☐ Eurydice

☐ Hermes

☐ Persephone

9. Which French writer lived with the composer Chopin?

☐ George Eliot

☐ Alfred de Musset

☐ Georges Simenon

☐ George Sand

10. What is the most abundant gas in the atmosphere?

☐ Methane

☐ Nitrogen

☐ Oxygen

☐ Ozone

ANSWERS

1 New Zealander. 2 Battle of the Boyne. 3 Bobby Robson. 4 Alva. 5 Oxygen. 6 Garfield. 7 Catholic Priest. 8 Eurydice. 9 George Sand. 10 Nitrogen.

237

QUIZ 116

1. Whose famous theorem is concerned with the sums of the squares of the sides of right-angled triangles?
- ☐ Aristotle
- ☐ Archimedes
- ☐ Pythagoras
- ☐ Zeux

2. What relation was Mary I to Elizabeth I?
- ☐ Daughter
- ☐ Half-sister
- ☐ Mother
- ☐ Sister

3. Which ocean lies to the north of Russia?
- ☐ Atlantic Ocean
- ☐ Arctic Ocean
- ☐ Antarctic Ocean
- ☐ Pacific Ocean

4. In which mythology does Yggdrasil feature?
- ☐ Arabian
- ☐ Greek
- ☐ Roman
- ☐ Scandinavian

5. What is Cortaderia selloana better known as?
- ☐ Grass
- ☐ Marijuana
- ☐ Pampas grass
- ☐ Potato

6. Of which ballet is Prince Siegfried hero?

☐ Cinderlla
☐ The Nutcracker
☐ The Ring
☐ Swan Lake

7. Who wrote _The Thorn Birds_?

☐ Taylor Caldwell
☐ Colleen McCullough
☐ Barbara Taylor Bradford
☐ Rachel Ward

8. Who was England's coach in Brazil 2014?

☐ Sven Goran Eriksson
☐ Glenn Hoddle
☐ Roy Hodgson
☐ Wayne Rooney

9. What is the boiling point of water on the Fahrenheit Scale?

☐ 100
☐ 150
☐ 212
☐ 451

10. Who was 007's boss?

☐ M
☐ Moneypenny
☐ P
☐ Q

1 Pythagoras. 2 Half-sister. 3 Arctic Ocean. 4 Scandinavian. 5 Pampas grass. 6 Swan Lake. 7 Colleen McCullough. 8 Roy Hodgson. 9 212. 10 M.

239

QUIZ 117

1. What was landscape gardener Capability Brown's real first name?
- [ ] Arthur
- [ ] Gavin
- [ ] Lancelot
- [ ] Merlin

2. How did Princess Grace of Monaco die?
- [ ] Car crash
- [ ] Plane crash
- [ ] She was shot
- [ ] Suicide

3. Which horror movie actor's real name is William Pratt?
- [ ] Lon Chaney, Jr
- [ ] Boris Karloff
- [ ] Bela Lugosi
- [ ] Vincent Price

4. Who famously said, "He is the very pineapple of politeness"?
- [ ] Winston Churchill
- [ ] Mrs Malaprop
- [ ] Edna Sharples
- [ ] Wodan

5. Who wrote *Paradise Postponed*?
- [ ] Wendy Craig
- [ ] Leo McKern
- [ ] John Milton
- [ ] John Mortimer

6. In which fictional county do the Archers live?

☐ Barsetshire
☐ Borsetshire
☐ Rutland
☐ Wessex

7. The poster advertising _Miss Saigon_ featured what type of transport?

☐ Car
☐ Helicopter
☐ Jeep
☐ Junk (boat)

8. Who wrote the book _William the Detective_?

☐ Mary Cadogan
☐ Richmal Crompton
☐ W.E. Johns
☐ Frank Richards

9. Which Russian city used to be called Leningrad?

☐ Moscow
☐ St Petersburg
☐ Stalingrad
☐ Volgograd

10. How many faces did the Romans believe Janus to have?

☐ 2
☐ 3
☐ 4
☐ 12

ANSWERS

1 Lancelot. 2 Car crash. 3 Boris Karloff. 4 Mrs Malaprop. 5 John Mortimer. 6 Borsetshire. 7 Helicopter. 8 Richmal Crompton. 9 St Petersburg. 10 2.

241

QUIZ 118

1. Which planet did Herschel discover in 1781?
- [ ] Jupiter
- [ ] Mars
- [ ] Pluto
- [ ] Uranus

2. How many atoms of oxygen are there in one molecule of water?
- [ ] 1
- [ ] 2
- [ ] 8
- [ ] 16

3. What was the title of the third *Lord of the Rings* movie?
- [ ] An Unexpected Journey
- [ ] Fellowship of the Ring
- [ ] The Return of the King
- [ ] The Two Towers

4. What does the "C" in TUC stand for?
- [ ] Chicken
- [ ] Club
- [ ] Congress
- [ ] Council

5. Who wrote the music for the *The Threepenny Opera*?
- [ ] Bertold Brecht
- [ ] Hanns Eisler
- [ ] Tom Waits
- [ ] Kurt Weill

6. What nationality was ballet star Rudolf Nureyev?

- [ ] American
- [ ] Estonian
- [ ] Russian
- [ ] Ukrainian

7. Who left an unfinished novel called *Sanditon*?

- [ ] Jane Austen
- [ ] George Eliot
- [ ] Elizabeth Gaskell
- [ ] Thomas Hardy

8. Name the odd one out?

- [ ] Fifty Shades Again
- [ ] Fifty Shades Darker
- [ ] Fifty Shades Freed
- [ ] Fifty Shades of Grey

9. Who carried the spirits of dead warriors to Valhalla?

- [ ] Norns
- [ ] Odin
- [ ] Thor
- [ ] Valkyrie

10. What were the initials of the Soviet secret police?

- [ ] CIA
- [ ] FTP
- [ ] KGB
- [ ] MI6

ANSWERS

1 Uranus. 2 1. 3 The Return of the King. 4 Congress. 5 Kurt Weill. 6 Russian. 7 Jane Austen. 8 Fifty Shades Again (it's not a real book). 9 Valkyrie. 10 KGB.

243

QUIZ 119

1. In the fiction what type of creature is the ballerina Angelina?

☐ Cat
☐ Dog
☐ Mouse
☐ Sheep

2. Which William was married to Mary II?

☐ William I
☐ William II
☐ William III
☐ William IV

3. In which TV programme did John Humphrys take over from Magnus Magnusson?

☐ Mastermind
☐ Newsnight
☐ Question Time
☐ The Today Programme

4. In Indian cuisine, what vegetable is referred to as "Aloo"?

☐ Okra
☐ Potato
☐ Spinach
☐ Tomato

5. If an elderly couple are happily married who or what are they likened to?

☐ Adam and Eve
☐ Brad and Angelina
☐ Darby and Joan
☐ Horse and carriage

6. Which sport is played at Rosslyn Park?

☐ Football
☐ Hockey
☐ Rugby League
☐ Rugby Union

7. How many cents are there in a US nickel?

☐ 1
☐ 5
☐ 10
☐ 25

8. With which country do you associate the drink Pernod?

☐ Belgium
☐ France
☐ Greece
☐ Russia

9. Of which country is Tripoli the capital?

☐ Algeria
☐ Egypt
☐ Libya
☐ Tunisia

10. How much in old money was a tanner?

☐ 6 pence
☐ 2 pence
☐ 10 pence
☐ 10 pounds

QUIZ 120

1. In which London park is the Serpentine?

☐ Hyde Park
☐ Queen Elizabeth Olympic Park
☐ Regent's Park
☐ St James's Park

2. Of which country is Baffin Island a part?

☐ Canada
☐ Greenland
☐ Iceland
☐ USA

3. Who wrote the novel *Lord of the Flies*?

☐ William Golding
☐ William Gibson
☐ Martin Pincher
☐ J.D. Salinger

4. What colour are the flowers of the hawthorn?

☐ Black or grey
☐ Orange
☐ Pink or yellow
☐ White or red

5. What is the common name for calcium carbonate?

☐ Chalk
☐ Cheese
☐ Salt
☐ Tar

6. What do we call what the Germans call "Strumpfhose"?

☐ Tights
☐ Trousers
☐ Stockings
☐ Socks

7. In chess, how many squares can the king move at a time?

☐ 1
☐ 2
☐ 3
☐ As many as it wants to

8. On what type of surface is the sport of curling played?

☐ Ice
☐ Grass
☐ Gravel
☐ Tarmac

9. Which French king was husband to Marie Antoinette?

☐ Louis XV
☐ Louis XVI
☐ Louis XVII
☐ Louis XVIII

10. What are bespoke clothes?

☐ Made for sports
☐ Made to measure
☐ Second hand
☐ Underwear

ANSWERS

1 Hyde Park. 2 Canada. 3 William Golding. 4 White or red. 5 Chalk. 6 Tights. 7 1. 8 Ice. 9 Louis XVI. 10 Made to measure.

247

QUIZ 121

1. According to the proverb, what shouldn't call the kettle black?
- ☐ The dish
- ☐ The fire
- ☐ The handle
- ☐ The pot

2. What sort of a holiday is it if you do the same thing as in your job?
- ☐ Busman's
- ☐ Dustman's
- ☐ Rubbish
- ☐ Vacation

3. What is a peruke?
- ☐ A bird
- ☐ A dog
- ☐ A hat
- ☐ A wig

4. What was Louis Armstrong's nickname?
- ☐ Bird
- ☐ Cheeky
- ☐ L'il Louis
- ☐ Satchmo

5. According to the proverb, what is better than no bread?
- ☐ A slice or two
- ☐ A whole loaf
- ☐ Half a loaf
- ☐ Half a slice

6. What kind of animal is a Persian Blue?

- ☐ Bird
- ☐ Cat
- ☐ Dog
- ☐ Pony

7. Who composed the opera *Carmen*?

- ☐ Beethoven
- ☐ Bizet
- ☐ Verdi
- ☐ Wagner

8. On a ship or boat what is a painter?

- ☐ An anchor chain
- ☐ A handyman
- ☐ A person with a paintbrush
- ☐ A rope

9. What condiment is manufactured by Lea & Perrins?

- ☐ HP Sauce
- ☐ Ketchup
- ☐ Mayonnaise
- ☐ Worcestershire Sauce

10. Where in London is the statue of Peter Pan?

- ☐ Buckingham Palace
- ☐ Green Park
- ☐ Hackney Downs
- ☐ Kensington Gardens

ANSWERS

9 Worcestershire Sauce. 10 Kensington Gardens.

1 Pot. 2 Businair's. 9 Wig. 4 Sacchino. 5 Half a loaf. 6 Cat. 7 Bizet. 8 Rope.

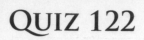

QUIZ 122

1. In geometry, what is meant by concentric?
☐ Being parallel
☐ Being the same shape
☐ Being the same size
☐ Having the same centre

2. Who first presented *The Antiques Roadshow* in 1979?
☐ Michael Aspel
☐ Arthur Negis
☐ Bruce Parker
☐ Hugh Scully

3. In which of Dickens's novels does Sam Weller appear?
☐ A Tale of Two Cities
☐ Domby and Son
☐ Oliver Twist
☐ The Pickwick Papers

4. Which food, not rationed during World War II, was rationed after it?
☐ Bacon
☐ Bread
☐ Eggs
☐ Milk

5. What is the name of the marmalade cat created by Kathleen Hale?
☐ Alexander
☐ Babar
☐ Melchior
☐ Orlando

6. For what is the Médoc area of France famous?

☐ Cheese
☐ Mountains
☐ Flowers
☐ Wine

7. Which is the odd one out?

☐ Cheshire
☐ Gouda
☐ Gorgonzola
☐ Surrey

8. As what did Beau Brummel achieve fame?

☐ Fashion leader
☐ Knitter
☐ Swordsman
☐ Trade unionist

9. Which country used to have a coin called a bawbee?

☐ England
☐ Ireland
☐ Scotland
☐ Wales

10. In London, the Cambridge, the Lyric and the Adelphi are all what?

☐ Hospitals
☐ Museums
☐ Parks
☐ Theatres

ANSWERS

1 Having the same centre. 2 Bruce Parker. 3 The Pickwick Papers. 4 Bread. 5 Orlando. 6 Wine. 7 Surrey (the others are types of cheese). 8 Fashion leader. 9 Scotland. 10 Theatres

251

QUIZ 123

1. Which religious writer was born in Elstow, near Bedford?
- [ ] John Bunyan
- [ ] Jonathan Edwards
- [ ] John Milton
- [ ] John Owen

2. In which year was the Gunpowder Plot?
- [ ] 1699
- [ ] 1600
- [ ] 1605
- [ ] 1666

3. What does a chandler make?
- [ ] Birdcages
- [ ] Candles
- [ ] Chairs
- [ ] Shoes

4. In which country did the poets Keats and Shelley both die?
- [ ] England
- [ ] Ireland
- [ ] Italy
- [ ] USA

5. How many tusks does a warthog have?
- [ ] 1
- [ ] 2
- [ ] 3
- [ ] 4

6. What is the nearest star to the solar system?

- ☐ Alpha Centauri
- ☐ Barnard's Star
- ☐ Proxima Centauri
- ☐ Sirius

7. Who was king of France at the time of the French Revolution?

- ☐ Louis XIV
- ☐ Louis XV
- ☐ Louis XVI
- ☐ Louis XVII

8. Which card game has two forms, called auction and contract?

- ☐ Bridge
- ☐ Canasta
- ☐ Hearts
- ☐ Poker

9. Graphite is composed of which element?

- ☐ Aluminium
- ☐ Carbon
- ☐ Iron
- ☐ Silver

10. Where was the Mount Pinatubo eruption?

- ☐ Italy
- ☐ Japan
- ☐ The Phillipines
- ☐ USA

ANSWERS

1 John Bunyan. 2 1605. 3 Candles. 4 Italy. 5 4. 6 Proxima Centauri. 7 Louis XVI. 8 Bridge. 9 Carbon. 10 The Philippines.

QUIZ 124

1. Which of the following does the equator NOT cross?
- [ ] Argentina
- [ ] Brazil
- [ ] Columbia
- [ ] Ecuador

2. What was the first X-rated film to win an Oscar?
- [ ] Citizen Kane
- [ ] Deep Throat
- [ ] The Godfather
- [ ] Midnight Cowboy

3. What did Little Polly Flinders spoil?
- [ ] Her appetite
- [ ] Her children
- [ ] Her milk
- [ ] Her nice new clothes

4. What metallic element is mixed with tin to form the alloy bronze?
- [ ] Aluminium
- [ ] Copper
- [ ] Iron
- [ ] Nickel

5. In which city did Karl Marx write *Das Kapital*?
- [ ] Berlin
- [ ] London
- [ ] Moscow
- [ ] New York

6. Who was world professional billiards champion from 1968 to 1980?

☐ John Pulman
☐ Ray Reardon
☐ John Spencer
☐ Rex Williams

7. Which New York baseball player married Marilyn Monroe?

☐ Joe DiMaggio
☐ Mickey Mantle
☐ Arthur Miller
☐ Babe Ruth

8. Which country is the world's leading producer of copper?

☐ Brazil
☐ Chile
☐ China
☐ Congo

9. Which country's flag shows a green star on a red background?

☐ Algeria
☐ Egypt
☐ Libya
☐ Morocco

10. Which was Madonna's first UK top ten hit?

☐ Borderline
☐ Holiday
☐ Like A Virgin
☐ Lucky Star

ANSWERS

1 Argentina. 2 Midnight Cowboy. 3 Her nice new clothes. 4 Copper. 5 London. 6 Rex Williams. 7 Joe DiMaggio. 8 Chile. 9 Morocco. 10 Holiday.

255

QUIZ NOTES